HERITAGE CLASSICS

William Shakespeare

Hamlet

HERITAGE

HERITAGE PUBLISHERS

NEW DELHI

HERITAGE PUBLISHERS
19-A, Ansari Road, Daryaganj, New Delhi-110002
Tel.: 23266258, 23264444
Fax: 23263050, E-mail: heritage@nda.vsnl.net.in

ISBN : 9788170262473

Printed in India
Sagar Printers, 23 Ansari Road
New Delhi-110002

About the Author

DETAILS about William Shakespeare's life are sketchy, mostly mere surmise based upon court or other clerical records. His parents, John and Mary (Arden), were married about 1557; she was of the landed gentry, he a yeoman—a glover and commodities merchant. By 1568, John had risen through the ranks of town government and held the position of high bailiff, similar to mayor. William, the eldest son, was born in 1564, probably on April 23, several days before his baptism on April 26, 1564. That Shakespeare also died on April 23, 52 years later, may have resulted in the adoption of this birthdate.

William no doubt attended the local grammar school in Stratford where his parents lived, and would have studied primarily Latin rhetoric, logic, and literature. At age 18 (1582), William married Anne Hathaway, a local farmer's daughter eight years his senior. Their first daughter, Susanna, was born six months later (1583), and twins Judith and Hamnet were born in 1585.

Shakespeare's life can be divided into three periods: the first 20 years in Stratford, which include his schooling, early marriage, and fatherhood; the next 25 years as an actor and playwright in London; and the last five in retirement back in Stratford where he enjoyed moderate wealth gained from his theatrical successes. The years linking the first two periods are marked by a lack of information about Shakespeare, and are often referred to as the "dark years"; the transition from active work into retirement was gradual and cannot be precisely dated.

John Shakespeare had suffered financial reverses from William's teen years until well into the height of the playwright's popularity and success. In 1596, John Shakespeare was granted a coat of arms, almost certainly purchased by William, who the next year bought a sizable house in Stratford. By the time of his death, William had substantial properties, both professional and personal, which he bestowed on his theatrical associates and his family (primarily his daughter Susanna, having rewritten his will one month before his death to protect his assets from Judith's new husband, Thomas Quiney, who ran afoul of church doctrine and public esteem before and after the marriage).

Shakespeare probably left school at 15, which was the norm, and took some sort of job, especially since this was the period of his father's financial difficulty. Numerous references in his plays suggest that William may have in fact worked for his father, thereby gaining specialized knowledge.

At some point during the "dark years," Shakespeare began his career with a London theatrical company—perhaps in 1589—for he was already an actor and playwright of some note in 1592. Shakespeare apparently wrote and acted for Pembroke's Men, as well as numerous others, in particular Strange's Men, which later became the Chamberlain's Men, with whom he remained for the rest of his career.

When, in 1592, the Plague closed the theaters for about two years, Shakespeare turned to writing book-length narrative poetry. Most notable were "Venus and Adonis" and "The Rape of Lucrece," both of which were dedicated to the Earl of Southampton, whom scholars accept as Shakespeare's friend and benefactor despite a lack of documentation. During the same period, Shakespeare was writing his sonnets, which are more likely signs of the time's fashion rather than actual love poems detailing any particular relationship. He returned to play writing when theaters reopened in 1594, and published no more poetry. His sonnets were published without his consent in 1609, shortly before his retirement.

Amid all of his success, Shakespeare suffered the loss of his only son, Hamnet, who died in 1596 at the age of 11. But Shakespeare's career continued unabated, and in London in 1599, he became one of the partners in the new Globe Theater, built by the Chamberlain's Men. This group was a remarkable assemblage of excellent actors who were also business partners and close personal friends . . . including Richard Burbage who all worked together as equals . . . .

When Queen Elizabeth died in 1603 and was succeeded by her cousin King James of Scotland, the Chamberlain's Men was renamed the King's Men, and Shakespeare's productivity and popularity continued uninterrupted. He invested in London real estate and, one year away from retirement, purchased a second theater, the Blackfriars Gatehouse, in partnership with his fellow actors. His final play was *Henry VIII*, two years before his death in 1616.

Incredibly, most of Shakespeare's plays had never been published in anything except pamphlet form, and were simply extant as acting scripts stored at the Globe. Only the efforts of two of Shakespeare's company, John Heminges and Henry Condell, preserved his 36 plays (minus *Pericles*, the thirty-seventh) in the First Folio. Heminges and Condell published the plays, they said, "only to keep the memory of so worthy a friend and fellow alive as was our Shakespeare". Theater scripts were not regarded as literary works of art, but only the basis for the performance. Plays were a popular form of entertainment for all layers of society in Shakespeare's time, which perhaps explains why Hamlet feels compelled to instruct the traveling Players on the fine points of acting, urging them not "to split the ears of the groundlings," nor "speak no more than is set down for them."

Present copies of Shakespeare's plays have, in some cases, been reconstructed in part from scripts written down by various members of an acting company who performed particular roles. Shakespeare's plays, like those of many of the actors who also were playwrights, belonged to the acting company. The performance, rather than the script, was what concerned the author, for that was how his play would become popular—and how the company, in which many actors were shareholders, would make money.

William Shakespeare died on April 23, 1616, and was buried two days later in the chancel of Holy Trinity Church where he had been baptized exactly 52 years earlier.

Plot Summary

THE PROTAGONIST of Hamlet is Prince Hamlet of Denmark, son of the recently deceased King Hamlet and the nephew of King Claudius, his father's brother and successor. After the death of King Hamlet, Claudius hastily marries King Hamlet's widow, Gertrude, Hamlet's mother. In the background is Denmark's long-standing feud with neighbouring Norway, and an invasion led by the Norwegian prince, Fortinbras, is expected.

The play opens on a cold night at Elsinore, the Danish royal castle. The sentries try to persuade Hamlet's friend Horatio that they have seen King Hamlet's ghost, when it appears again. After hearing from Horatio of the Ghost's appearance, Hamlet resolves to see the Ghost himself. That night, the Ghost appears to Hamlet. He tells Hamlet that he is the spirit of his father, and discloses that Claudius murdered King Hamlet by pouring poison in his ears. The Ghost demands that Hamlet avenge him; Hamlet agrees and decides to feign madness to avert suspicion. He is, however, uncertain of the Ghost's reliability.

Hamlet remains unconvinced that the Ghost has told him the truth, but the arrival of a troupe of actors at Elsinore presents him with a solution. He will stage a play, re-enacting his father's murder, and determine Claudius' guilt or innocence by studying his reaction. The Court assembles to watch the play; Hamlet provides a running commentary throughout. During the play, Claudius abruptly rises and leaves the room, which Hamlet sees as proof of his uncle's guilt. Claudius, fearing for his life, banishes Hamlet to England on a pretext, closely watched by Rosencrantz and Guildenstern, with a letter instructing that the bearer be killed.

Gertrude summons Hamlet to her closet to demand an explanation. On his way, Hamlet passes Claudius in prayer but hesitates to kill him, reasoning that death in prayer would send him to heaven. In the bedchamber, a row erupts between Hamlet and Gertrude. Polonius, spying hidden behind an arras, makes a noise; and Hamlet, believing it is Claudius, stabs wildly, killing Polonius. The Ghost appears, urging Hamlet to treat Gertrude gently but reminding him to kill Claudius.

Demented by grief at Polonius' death, Ophelia wanders Elsinore singing bawdy songs. Her brother, Laertes, arrives back from France, enraged by his father's death and his sister's madness. Claudius convinces Laertes that Hamlet is solely responsible; then news arrives that Hamlet is still at large. Claudius swiftly concocts a plot. He proposes a fencing match between Laertes and Hamlet in which Laertes will fight with a poison-tipped sword, but tacitly plans to offer Hamlet poisoned wine if that fails. Gertrude interrupts to report that Ophelia has drowned.

Two gravediggers discuss Ophelia's apparent suicide, while digging her grave. Hamlet arrives with Horatio and banters with a gravedigger, who unearths the skull of a jester from Hamlet's childhood, Yorick. Ophelia's funeral procession approaches, led by Laertes. He and Hamlet grapple, but the brawl is broken up.

Back at Elsinore, Hamlet tells Horatio how he escaped and that Rosencrantz and Guildenstern are dead. A courtier, Osric, interrupts to invite Hamlet to fence with Laertes. With Fortinbras' army closing on Elsinore, the match begins. Laertes pierces Hamlet with a poisoned blade but is fatally wounded by it himself. Gertrude drinks the poisoned wine and dies. In his dying moments, Laertes is reconciled with Hamlet and reveals Claudius' murderous plot. In his own last moments, Hamlet manages to kill Claudius and names Fortinbras as his heir. When Fortinbras arrives, Horatio recounts the tale and Fortinbras orders Hamlet's body borne off in honour.

The Tragedy of Hamlet, Prince of Denmark

The Actors' Names

CLAUDIUS, King of Denmark
HAMLET, Son to the late, and nephew to the present King
POLONIUS, Lord Chamberlain
HORATIO, Friend to Hamlet
LAERTES, Son to Polonius

VOLTIMAND CORNELIUS ROSENCRANTZ GUILDENSTERN OSRIC A Gentleman	Courtiers

A Priest

MARCELLUS BERNARDO FRANCISCO	Soldiers

REYNALDO, Servant to Polonius
The Players
Two Clowns, grave-diggers
FORTINBRAS, Prince of Norway
A Captain
English Ambassadors
GERTRUDE, Queen of Denmark, and mother to Hamlet
OPHELIA, daughter to Plonius
GHOST of Hamlet's Father

I. 1

Enter Bernardo and Francisco, two sentinels

BERNARDO: Who's there?
FRANCISCO: Nay, answer me: stand, and unfold yourself.
BERNARDO: Long live the King!
FRANCISCO: Bernardo?
BERNARDO: He.
FRANCISCO: You come most carefully upon your hour.
BERNARDO: 'Tis now struck twelve; get thee to bed, Francisco.
FRANCISCO: For this relief much thanks: 'tis bitter cold,
And I am sick at heart.
BERNARDO: Have you had quiet guard?
FRANCISCO: Not a mouse stirring.
BERNARDO: Well, good night.
If you do meet Horatio and Marcellus,
The rivals of my watch, bid them make haste.

Enter Horatio and Marcellus

FRANCISCO: I think I hear them. Stand, ho! Who's there?
HORATIO: Friends to this ground.
MARCELLUS: And liegemen to the Dane.
FRANCISCO: Give you good night.
MARCELLUS: O, farewell, honest soldiers:

Who hath relieved you?

FRANCISCO: Bernardo has my place.
Give you good night.

Exit Francisco.

MARCELLUS: Holla! Bernardo!

BERNARDO: Say, what, is Horatio there?

HORATIO: A piece of him.

BERNARDO: Welcome Horatio: welcome, good Marcellus.

MARCELLUS: What, has this thing appear'd again to-night?

BERNARDO: I have seen nothing.

MARCELLUS: Horatio says 'tis but our fantasy,
And will not let belief take hold of him
Touching this dreaded sight, twice seen of us:
Therefore I have entreated him along
With us, to watch the minutes of this night;
That if again this apparition come,
He may approve our eyes and speak to it.

HORATIO: Tush, tush, 'twill not appear.

BERNARDO: Sit down awhile;
And let us once again assail your ears,
That are so fortified against our story,
What we two nights have seen.

HORATIO: Well, sit we down,
And let us hear Bernardo speak of this.

BERNARDO: Last night of all,

When yond same star that's westward from the pole
Had made his course to illume that part of heaven
Where now it burns, Marcellus and myself,
The bell then beating one,

Enter Ghost

MARCELLUS: Peace, break thee off; look, where it comes again!

BERNARDO: In the same figure, like the King that's dead.

MARCELLUS: Thou art a scholar; speak to it, Horatio.

BERNARDO: Looks it not like the King? Mark it, Horatio.

HORATIO: Most like: it harrows me with fear and wonder.

BERNARDO: It would be spoke to.

MARCELLUS: Question it, Horatio.

HORATIO: What art thou that usurp'st this time of night,
Together with that fair and warlike form
In which the majesty of buried Denmark
Did sometimes march: by heaven I charge thee, speak!

MARCELLUS: It is offended.

BERNARDO: See, it stalks away!

HORATIO: Stay! speak, speak! I charge thee, speak!

Exit Ghost

MARCELLUS: 'Tis gone, and will not answer.

BERNARDO: How now, Horatio! you tremble and look pale:
Is not this something more than fantasy?
What think you on't?

HORATIO: Before my God, I might not this believe
Without the sensible and true avouch
Of mine own eyes.

MARCELLUS: Is it not like the King?

HORATIO: As thou art to thyself:
Such was the very armour he had on
When he the ambitious Norway combated;
So frown'd he once, when, in an angry parle,
He smote the sledded Poleaxe on the ice.
'Tis strange.

MARCELLUS: Thus twice before, and jump at this dead hour,
With martial stalk hath he gone by our watch.

HORATIO: In what particular thought to work I know not;
But in the gross and scope of my opinion,
This bodes some strange eruption to our State.

MARCELLUS: Good now, sit down, and tell me, he that knows,
Why this same strict and most observant watch,
So nightly toils the subject of the land,
And why such daily cast of brazen cannon,
And foreign mart for implements of war;
Why such impress of shipwrights, whose sore task
Does not divide the Sunday from the week;
What might be toward, that this sweaty haste

Doth make the night joint-labourer with the day:
Who is't that can inform me?
HORATIO: That can I;
At least, the whisper goes so. Our last King,
Whose image even but now appear'd to us,
Was, as you know, by Fortinbras of Norway,
(Thereto prick'd on by a most emulate pride,)
Dar'd to the combat; in which our valiant Hamlet
(For so this side of our known world esteem'd him)
Did slay this Fortinbras; who by a seal'd compact,
Well ratified by law and heraldry,
Did forfeit, with his life, all those his lands
Which he stood seized of, to the conqueror:
Against the which, a moiety competent
Was gaged by our King; which had return'd
To the inheritance of Fortinbras,
Had he been vanquisher; as, by the same cov'nant,
And carriage of the article design'd,
His fell to Hamlet. Now, sir, young Fortinbras,
Of unimproved mettle, hot and full,
Hath in the skirts of Norway, here and there
Shark'd up a list of lawless resolutes,
For food and diet, to some enterprise
That hath a stomach in't; which is no other
(As it doth well appear unto our state)
But to recover of us, by strong hand

And terms compulsatory, those foresaid lands
So by his father lost: and this, I take it,
Is the main motive of our preparations,
The source of this our watch and the chief head
Of this post-haste and romage in the land.
BERNARDO: I think it be no other, but e'en so:
Well may it sort that this portentous figure
Comes armed through our watch; so like the King
That was and is the question of these wars.
HORATIO: A mote it is to trouble the mind's eye.
In the most high and palmy state of Rome,
A little ere the mightiest Julius fell,
The graves stood tenantless and the sheeted dead
Did squeak and gibber in the Roman streets:
As stars with trains of fire and dews of blood,
Disasters in the sun; and the moist star
Upon whose influence Neptune's empire stands
Was sick almost to doomsday with eclipse:
And even the like precurse of fierce events,
As harbingers preceding still the fates
And prologue to the omen coming on,
Have heaven and earth together demonstrated
Unto our climatures and countrymen.
But soft, behold! lo, where it comes again!

Re-enter Ghost

I'll cross it, though it blast me. Stay, illusion!

If thou hast any sound, or use of voice,
Speak to me: If there be any good thing to be done,
That may to thee do ease and grace to me,
Speak to me:
If thou art privy to thy country's fate,
Which, happily, foreknowing may avoid, O, speak!
Or if thou hast uphoarded in thy life
Extorted treasure in the womb of earth,
For which, they say, you spirits oft walk in death,

The Cock crows

Speak of it: stay, and speak! Stop it, Marcellus.
MARCELLUS: Shall I strike at it with my partisan?
HORATIO: Do, if it will not stand.
BERNARDO: 'Tis here!
HORATIO: 'Tis here!

Exit Ghost

MARCELLUS: 'Tis gone!
We do it wrong, being so majestical,
To offer it the show of violence;
For it is, as the air, invulnerable,
And our vain blows malicious mockery.
BERNARDO: It was about to speak, when the cock crew.
HORATIO: And then it started like a guilty thing
Upon a fearful summons. I have heard,
The cock, that is the trumpet to the morn,
Doth with his lofty and shrill-sounding throat

Awake the god of day; and, at his warning,
Whether in sea or fire, in earth or air,
Th' extravagant and erring spirit hies
To his confine: and of the truth herein,
This present object made probation.

MARCELLUS: It faded on the crowing of the cock.
Some say that ever 'gainst that season comes
Wherein our Saviour's birth is celebrated,
The bird of dawning singeth all night long:
And then, they say, no spirit dares stir abroad;
The nights are wholesome; then no planets strike,
No fairy takes, nor witch hath power to charm,
So hallow'd and so gracious is the time.

HORATIO: So have I heard, and do in part believe it.
But, look, the morn, in russet mantle clad,
Walks o'er the dew of yon high eastern hill:
Break we our watch up; and by my advice,
Let us impart what we have seen to-night
Unto young Hamlet; for, upon my life,
This spirit, dumb to us, will speak to him.
Do you consent we shall acquaint him with it,
As needful in our loves, fitting our duty?

MARCELLUS: Let's do't, I pray; and I this morning know
Where we shall find him most conveniently.

Exeunt

I. 2

Flourish. Enter King Claudius, Queen Gertrude, Hamlet, Polonius, Laertes, Voltemand, Cornelius, Lords, and Attendants

KING: Though yet of Hamlet our dear brother's death
The memory be green, and that it us befitted
To bear our hearts in grief and our whole kingdom
To be contracted in one brow of woe,
Yet so far hath discretion fought with nature,
That we with wisest sorrow think on him,
Together with remembrance of ourselves.
Therefore our sometimes sister, now our Queen,
Th' imperial jointress to this warlike state,
Have we, as 'twere with a defeated joy,
With an auspicious and a dropping eye,
With mirth in funeral and with dirge in marriage,
In equal scale weighing delight and dole,
Taken to wife: nor have we herein barr'd
Your better wisdoms, which have freely gone
With this affair along. For all, our thanks.
Now follows, that you know, young Fortinbras,
Holding a weak supposal of our worth,
Or thinking by our late dear brother's death
Our state to be disjoint and out of frame,
Colleagued with the dream of his advantage,
He hath not fail'd to pester us with message,
Importing the surrender of those lands

Lost by his father, with all bonds of law,
To our most valiant brother. So much for him.
Now for ourself and for this time of meeting:
Thus much the business is: we have here writ
To Norway, uncle of young Fortinbras,
Who, impotent and bed-rid, scarcely hears
Of this his nephew's purpose, to suppress
His further gait herein; in that the levies,
The lists and full proportions, are all made
Out of his subject: and we here dispatch
You, good Cornelius, and you, Voltemand,
For bearers of this greeting to old Norway;
Giving to you no further personal power
To business with the king, more than the scope
Of these delated articles allow:
Farewell, and let your haste commend your duty.

VOLTEMAND: In that and all things, will we show our duty.

KING: We doubt it nothing: heartily farewell.

Exeunt Voltemand and Cornelius

And now, Laertes, what's the news with you?
You told us of some suit; what is't, Laertes?
You cannot speak of reason to the Dane,
And lose your voice: what wouldst thou beg, Laertes,
That shall not be my offer, not thy asking?
The head is not more native to the heart,
The hand more instrumental to the mouth,

Than is the throne of Denmark to thy father.
What wouldst thou have, Laertes?

LAERTES: My dread Lord,
Your leave and favour to return to France;
From whence though willingly I came to Denmark,
To show my duty in your Coronation,
Yet now, I must confess, that duty done,
My thoughts and wishes bend again toward France,
And bow them to your gracious leave and pardon.

KING: Have you your father's leave? What says Polonius?

POLONIUS: He hath, my Lord, wrung from me my slow leave
By laboursome petition, and at last
Upon his will I seal'd my hard consent:
I do beseech you, give him leave to go.

KING: Take thy fair hour, Laertes; time be thine,
And thy best graces spend it at thy will!
But now, my cousin Hamlet, and my son,

HAMLET: A little more than kin, and less than kind.

KING: How is it that the clouds still hang on you?

HAMLET: Not so, my Lord; I am too much i' th' sun.

QUEEN: Good Hamlet, cast thy nighted colour off,
And let thine eye look like a friend on Denmark.
Do not for ever with thy vailed lids
Seek for thy noble father in the dust:

Thou know'st 'tis common; all that lives must die,
Passing through nature to eternity.
HAMLET: Ay, Madam, it is common.
QUEEN: If it be,
Why seems it so particular with thee?
HAMLET: Seems, Madam! nay it is; I know not seems.
'Tis not alone my inky cloak, good mother,
Nor customary suits of solemn black,
Nor windy suspiration of forced breath,
No, nor the fruitful river in the eye,
Nor the dejected 'havior of the visage,
Together with all forms, moods, shapes of grief,
That can denote me truly: these indeed seem,
For they are actions that a man might play:
But I have that within which passeth show;
These, but the trappings and the suits of woe.
KING: 'Tis sweet and commendable in your nature, Hamlet,
To give these mourning duties to your father:
But, you must know, your father lost a father;
That father lost, lost his, and the survivor bound
In filial obligation for some term
To do obsequious sorrow: but to persever
In obstinate condolement is a course
Of impious stubborness; 'tis unmanly grief;
It shows a will most incorrect to heaven,

A heart unfortified, a mind impatient,
An understanding simple and unschool'd:
For what we know must be and is as common
As any the most vulgar thing to sense,
Why should we in our peevish opposition
Take it to heart? Fie! 'tis a fault to heaven,
A fault against the dead, a fault to nature,
To reason most absurd: whose common theme
Is death of fathers, and who still hath cried,
From the first corse till he that died to-day,
'This must be so.' We pray you, throw to earth
This unprevailing woe, and think of us
As of a father: for let the world take note,
You are the most immediate to our Throne;
And with no less nobility of love
Than that which dearest father bears his son,
Do I impart toward you. For your intent
In going back to school in Wittenberg,
It is most retrograde to our desire:
And we beseech you, bend you to remain
Here, in the cheer and comfort of our eye,
Our chiefest courtier, cousin, and our son.
QUEEN: Let not thy mother lose her prayers, Hamlet:
I pray thee, stay with us; go not to Wittenberg.
HAMLET: I shall in all my best obey you, Madam.
KING: Why, 'tis a loving and a fair reply:

Be as ourself in Denmark. Madam, come;
This gentle and unforced accord of Hamlet
Sits smiling to my heart: in grace whereof,
No jocund health that Denmark drinks to-day,
But the great cannon to the clouds shall tell,
And the King's rouse the heavens all bruit again,
Re-speaking earthly thunder. Come away.

Exeunt all but Hamlet

HAMLET: O, that this too too solid flesh, would melt,
Thaw and resolve itself into a dew!
Or that the Everlasting had not fix'd
His canon 'gainst self-slaughter! O God! O God!
How weary, stale, flat and unprofitable,
Seem to me all the uses of this world!
Fie on't! oh fie! 'tis an unweeded garden,
That grows to seed; things rank and gross in nature
Possess it merely. That it should come to this!
But two months dead: nay, not so much, not two:
So excellent a King; that was, to this,
Hyperion to a satyr; so loving to my mother,
That he might not beteem the winds of heaven
Visit her face too roughly. Heaven and earth!
Must I remember? Why, she would hang on him,
As if increase of appetite had grown
By what it fed on: and yet, within a month
Let me not think on't: Frailty, thy name is woman!

A little month, or ere those shoes were old
With which she follow'd my poor father's body,
Like Niobe, all tears: why she, even she
O, God! a beast, that wants discourse of reason,
Would have mourn'd longer married with my uncle,
My father's brother, but no more like my father
Than I to Hercules: within a month:
Ere yet the salt of most unrighteous tears
Had left the flushing of her galled eyes,
She married. O, most wicked speed, to post
With such dexterity to incestuous sheets!
It is not, nor it cannot come to good:
But break, my heart; for I must hold my tongue.

Enter Horatio, Marcellus, and Bernardo

HORATIO: Hail to your lordship!

HAMLET: I am glad to see you well:
Horatio, or I do forget myself.

HORATIO: The same, my Lord, and your poor servant ever.

HAMLET: Sir, my good friend; I'll change that name with you:
And what make you from Wittenberg, Horatio? Marcellus?

MARCELLUS: My good Lord.

HAMLET: I am very glad to see you. Good even, sir.
But what, in faith, make you from Wittenberg?

HORATIO: A truant disposition, good my Lord.
HAMLET: I would not hear your enemy say so,
Nor shall you do mine ear that violence,
To make it truster of your own report
Against yourself: I know you are no truant:
But what is your affair in Elsinore?
We'll teach you to drink deep ere you depart.
HORATIO: My Lord, I came to see your father's funeral.
HAMLET: I pray thee, do not mock me, fellow-student;
I think it was to see my mother's wedding.
HORATIO: Indeed, my Lord, it follow'd hard upon.
HAMLET: Thrift, thrift, Horatio! the funeral baked meats
Did coldly furnish forth the marriage tables.
Would I had met my dearest foe in heaven
Or ever I had seen that day, Horatio!
My father! methinks I see my father.
HORATIO: Where, my Lord?
HAMLET: In my mind's eye, Horatio.
HORATIO: I saw him once; he was a goodly King.
HAMLET: He was a man, take him for all in all,
I shall not look upon his like again.
HORATIO: My Lord, I think I saw him yesternight.
HAMLET: Saw? Who?
HORATIO: My Lord, the King your father.
HAMLET: The King my father?
HORATIO: Season your admiration for awhile

With an attent ear, till I may deliver,
Upon the witness of these gentlemen,
This marvel to you.

HAMLET: For God's love, let me hear.

HORATIO: Two nights together had these gentlemen,
Marcellus and Bernardo, on their watch,
In the dead vast and middle of the night,
Been thus encounter'd. A figure like your father,
Armed at point exactly, cap-a-pe,
Appears before them, and with solemn march
Goes slow and stately by them: thrice he walk'd
By their oppress'd and fear-surprised eyes,
Within his truncheon's length; whilst they, distilled
Almost to jelly with the act of fear,
Stand dumb and speak not to him. This to me
In dreadful secrecy impart they did;
And I with them the third night kept the watch;
Where, as they had deliver'd, both in time,
Form of the thing, each word made true and good,
The apparition comes: I knew your father;
These hands are not more like.

HAMLET: But where was this?

MARCELLUS: My Lord, upon the platform where we watch'd.

HAMLET: Did you not speak to it?

HORATIO: My Lord, I did;

But answer made it none: yet once methought
It lifted up its head and did address
Itself to motion, like as it would speak;
But even then the morning cock crew loud,
And at the sound it shrunk in haste away,
And vanish'd from our sight.

HAMLET:'Tis very strange.

HORATIO: As I do live, my honour'd Lord, 'tis true;
And we did think it writ down in our duty
To let you know of it.

HAMLET: Indeed, indeed, sirs, but this troubles me.
Hold you the watch to-night?

BOTH: We do, my Lord.

HAMLET: Arm'd, say you?

BOTH: Arm'd, my Lord.

HAMLET: From top to toe?

BOTH: My Lord, from head to foot.

HAMLET: Then saw you not his face?

HORATIO: O, yes, my Lord; he wore his beaver up.

HAMLET: What, look'd he frowningly?

HORATIO: A countenance more in sorrow than in anger.

HAMLET: Pale or red?

HORATIO: Nay, very pale.

HAMLET: And fix'd his eyes upon you?

HORATIO: Most constantly.

HAMLET: I would I had been there.

HORATIO: It would have much amazed you.
HAMLET: Very like, very like. Stay'd it long?
HORATIO: While one with moderate haste might tell a hundred.
BOTH: Longer, longer.
HORATIO: Not when I saw't.
HAMLET: His beard was grizzled, no?
HORATIO: It was, as I have seen it in his life,
A sable silver'd.
HAMLET: I will watch to-night;
Perchance 'twill walk again.
HORATIO: I warrant you it will.
HAMLET: If it assume my noble father's person,
I'll speak to it, though hell itself should gape
And bid me hold my peace. I pray you all,
If you have hitherto conceal'd this sight,
Let it be tenable in your silence still;
And whatsoever else shall hap to-night,
Give it an understanding, but no tongue:
I will requite your loves. So, fare you well:
Upon the platform, 'twixt eleven and twelve,
I'll visit you.
ALL: Our duty to your Honour.
HAMLET: Your loves, as mine to you: farewell.

Exeunt all but Hamlet

My father's spirit in arms! all is not well;

I doubt some foul play: would the night were come!
Till then sit still, my soul: foul deeds will rise,
Though all the earth o'erwhelm them, to men's eyes.

Exit

I. 3

Enter Laertes and Ophelia

LAERTES: My necessaries are embark'd: farewell:
And, sister, as the winds give benefit
And convoy is assistant, do not sleep,
But let me hear from you.

OPHELIA: Do you doubt that?

LAERTES: For Hamlet and the trifling of his favour,
Hold it a fashion and a toy in blood,
A violet in the youth of primy nature,
Forward, not permanent, sweet, not lasting,
The perfume and suppliance of a minute; no more.

OPHELIA: No more but so?

LAERTES: Think it no more;
For nature, crescent does not grow alone
In thews and bulk but, as this temple waxes,
The inward service of the mind and soul
Grows wide withal. Perhaps he loves you now,
And now no soil nor cautel doth besmirch
The virtue of his will: but you must fear,

His greatness weigh'd, his will is not his own;
For he himself is subject to his birth:
He may not, as unvalued persons do,
Carve for himself; for on his choice depends
The sanctity and health of this whole State;
And therefore must his choice be circumscribed
Unto the voice and yielding of that body,
Whereof he is the head. Then if he says he loves you,
It fits your wisdom so far to believe it
As he in his particular act and place
May give his saying deed; which is no further
Than the main voice of Denmark goes withal.
Then weigh what loss your honour may sustain,
If with too credent ear you list his songs,
Or lose your heart, or your chaste treasure open
To his unmaster'd importunity.
Fear it, Ophelia, fear it, my dear sister,
And keep you in the rear of your affection,
Out of the shot and danger of desire.
The chariest maid is prodigal enough,
If she unmask her beauty to the moon:
Virtue itself 'scapes not calumnious strokes:
The canker galls the infants of the spring,
Too oft before their buttons be disclos'd,
And in the morn and liquid dew of youth
Contagious blastments are most imminent.

Be wary then; best safety lies in fear:
Youth to itself rebels, though none else near.
OPHELIA: I shall th' effect of this good lesson keep,
As watchman to my heart. But, good my brother,
Do not, as some ungracious pastors do,
Show me the steep and thorny way to heaven;
Whiles, like a puff'd and reckless libertine,
Himself the primrose path of dalliance treads,
And wrecks not his own rede.
LAERTES: O, fear me not.

Enter Polonius

I stay too long: but here my father comes.
A double blessing is a double grace,
Occasion smiles upon a second leave.
POLONIUS: Yet here, Laertes! aboard, aboard, for shame!
The wind sits in the shoulder of your sail,
And you are stay'd for. There; my blessing with thee!
And these few precepts in thy memory
See thou character. Give thy thoughts no tongue,
Nor any unproportioned thought his act.
Be thou familiar, but by no means vulgar.
Those friends thou hast, and their adoption tried,
Grapple them to thy soul with hoops of steel;
But do not dull thy palm with entertainment
Of each new-hatch'd, unfledged comrade. Beware
Of entrance to a quarrel, but being in,

Bear't that th' opposed may beware of thee.
Give every man thine ear, but few thy voice;
Take each man's censure, but reserve thy judgment.
Costly thy habit as thy purse can buy,
But not express'd in fancy; rich, not gaudy;
For the apparel oft proclaims the man,
And they in France of the best rank and station
Or of a most select and generous chief in that.
Neither a borrower nor a lender be;
For loan oft loses both itself and friend,
And borrowing dulls the edge of husbandry.
This above all: to thine ownself be true,
And it must follow, as the night the day,
Thou canst not then be false to any man.
Farewell: my blessing season this in thee!

LAERTES: Most humbly do I take my leave, my Lord.

POLONIUS: The time invites you; go; your servants tend.

LAERTES: Farewell, Ophelia; and remember well
What I have said to you.

OPHELIA: 'Tis in my memory lock'd,
And you yourself shall keep the key of it.

LAERTES: Farewell.

Exeunt

POLONIUS: What is't, Ophelia, be hath said to you?

OPHELIA: So please you, something touching the Lord Hamlet.

POLONIUS: Marry, well bethought:
'Tis told me, he hath very oft of late
Given private time to you; and you yourself
Have of your audience been most free and bounteous:
If it be so, as so 'tis put on me,
And that in way of caution, I must tell you,
You do not understand yourself so clearly
As it behoves my daughter and your honour.
What is between you, give me up the truth.

OPHELIA: He hath, my Lord, of late made many tenders
Of his affection to me.

POLONIUS: Affection! pooh! you speak like a green girl,
Unsifted in such perilous circumstance.
Do you believe his tenders, as you call them?

OPHELIA: I do not know, my Lord, what I should think.

POLONIUS: Marry, I'll teach you: think yourself a baby;
That you have ta'en these tenders for true pay,
Which are not sterling. Tender yourself more dearly;
Or not to crack the wind of the poor phrase,
Running it thus you'll tender me a fool.

OPHELIA: My Lord, he hath importun'd me with love
In honourable fashion.

POLONIUS: Ay, fashion you may call it; go to, go to.

OPHELIA: And hath given countenance to his speech, my Lord,
With almost all the holy vows of heaven.

POLONIUS: Ay, springes to catch woodcocks. I do know,
When the blood burns, how prodigal the soul
Lends the tongue vows: these blazes, daughter,
Giving more light than heat, extinct in both,
Even in their promise, as it is a-making,
You must not take for fire. From this time
Be somewhat scanter of your maiden presence;
Set your entreatments at a higher rate
Than a command to parley. For Lord Hamlet,
Believe so much in him, that he is young
And with a larger tether may he walk,
Than may be given you: in few, Ophelia,
Do not believe his vows; for they are brokers,
Not of that dye which their investments show,
But mere implorators of unholy suits,
Breathing like sanctified and pious bawds,
The better to beguile. This is for all:
I would not, in plain terms, from this time forth,
Have you so slander any moment leisure,
As to give words or talk with the Lord Hamlet.
Look to't, I charge you: come your ways.
OPHELIA: I shall obey, my Lord.

Exeunt

I. 4

Enter Hamlet, Horatio, and Marcellus

HAMLET: The air bites shrewdly; it is very cold.

HORATIO: It is a nipping and an eager air.

HAMLET: What hour now?

HORATIO: I think it lacks of twelve.

HAMLET: No, it is struck.

MARCELLUS: Indeed? I heard it not: then it draws near the season,
Wherein the spirit held his wont to walk.

A flourish of trumpets, and two pieces go off.

What does this mean, my Lord?

HAMLET: The King doth wake to-night and takes his rouse,
Keeps wassail, and the swaggering up-spring reels;
And, as he drains his draughts of Rhenish down,
The kettle-drum and trumpet thus bray out
The triumph of his pledge.

HORATIO: Is it a custom?

HAMLET: Ay, marry, is't:
But to my mind, though I am native here,
And to the manner born, it is a custom
More honour'd in the breach than the observance.
This heavy-headed revel east and west
Makes us traduc'd and tax'd of other nations:
They clepe us drunkards, and with swinish phrase

Soil our addition; and indeed it takes
From our achievements, though perform'd at height,
The pith and marrow of our attribute.
So, oft it chances in particular men,
That for some vicious mole of nature in them,
As, in their birth wherein they are not guilty,
Since nature cannot choose his origin
By their o'ergrowth of some complexion,
Oft breaking down the pales and forts of reason,
Or by some habit that too much o'er-leavens
The form of plausive manners, that these men,
Carrying, I say, the stamp of one defect,
Being nature's livery, or fortune's star,
Their virtues else be they as pure as grace,
As infinite as man may undergo
Shall in the general censure take corruption
From that particular fault: the dram of eale
Doth all the noble substance of a doubt
To his own scandal.

Enter Ghost

HORATIO: Look, my Lord, it comes!

HAMLET: Angels and ministers of grace defend us!
Be thou a spirit of health or goblin damn'd,
Bring with thee airs from heaven or blasts from hell,
Be thy intents wicked or charitable,
Thou com'st in such a questionable shape

That I will speak to thee: I'll call thee Hamlet,
King, father, royal Dane: O, answer me!
Let me not burst in ignorance; but tell
Why thy canoniz'd bones, hearsed in death,
Have burst their cerements; why the sepulchre,
Wherein we saw thee quietly inurn'd,
Hath op'd his ponderous and marble jaws,
To cast thee up again. What may this mean?
That thou, dead corse, again in complete steel,
Revisit'st thus the glimpses of the moon,
Making night hideous; and we fools of nature,
So horridly to shake our disposition
With thoughts beyond the reaches of our souls?
Say, why is this? wherefore? What should we do?

Ghost beckons Hamlet

HORATIO: It beckons you to go away with it,
As if it some impartment did desire
To you alone.

MARCELLUS: Look, with what courteous action
It wafts you to a more removed ground:
But do not go with it.

HORATIO: No, by no means.

HAMLET: It will not speak; then I will follow it.

HORATIO: Do not, my Lord.

HAMLET: Why, what should be the fear?
I do not set my life in a pin's fee;

And for my soul, what can it do to that,
Being a thing immortal as itself?
It waves me forth again: I'll follow it.

HORATIO: What if it tempt you toward the flood, my Lord,
Or to the dreadful summit of the cliff
That beetles o'er his base into the sea,
And there assume some other horrible form,
Which might deprive your sovereignty of reason
And draw you into madness? Think of it:
The very place puts toys of desperation,
Without more motive, into every brain
That looks so many fathoms to the sea
And hears it roar beneath.

HAMLET: It wafts me still.
Go on; I'll follow thee.

MARCELLUS: You shall not go, my Lord.

HAMLET: Hold off your hands.

HORATIO: Be ruled; you shall not go.

HAMLET: My fate cries out,
And makes each petty artery in this body
As hardy as the Nemean lion's nerve.
Still am I call'd. Unhand me, gentlemen.
By heaven, I'll make a ghost of him that lets me!
I say, away! Go on; I'll follow thee.

Exeunt Ghost and Hamlet

HORATIO: He waxes desperate with imagination.

MARCELLUS: Let's follow; 'tis not fit thus to obey him.

HORATIO: Have after. To what issue will this come?

MARCELLUS: Something is rotten in the state of Denmark.

HORATIO: Heaven will direct it.

MARCELLUS: Nay, let's follow him.

Exeunt

I. 5

Enter Ghost and Hamlet

HAMLET: Where wilt thou lead me? Speak; I'll go no further.

GHOST: Mark me.

HAMLET: I will.

GHOST: My hour is almost come,
When I to sulphurous and tormenting flames
Must render up myself.

HAMLET: Alas, poor ghost!

GHOST: Pity me not, but lend thy serious hearing
To what I shall unfold.

HAMLET: Speak; I am bound to hear.

GHOST: So art thou to revenge, when thou shalt hear.

HAMLET: What?

GHOST: I am thy father's spirit,
Doom'd for a certain term to walk the night,
And for the day confined to fast in fires,

Till the foul crimes done in my days of nature
Are burnt and purged away. But that I am forbid
To tell the secrets of my prison-house,
I could a-tale unfold whose lightest word
Would harrow up thy soul, freeze thy young blood,
Make thy two eyes, like stars, start from their spheres,
Thy knotted and combined locks to part
And each particular hair to stand on end,
Like quills upon the fretful porpentine:
But this eternal blazon must not be
To ears of flesh and blood. List, list, O, list!
If thou didst ever thy dear father love.

HAMLET: O God!

GHOST: Revenge his foul and most unnatural murder.

HAMLET: Murder!

GHOST: Murder most foul, as in the best it is;
But this most foul, strange and unnatural.

HAMLET: Haste me to know't, that I, with wings as swift
As meditation or the thoughts of love,
May sweep to my revenge.

GHOST: I find thee apt;
And duller shouldst thou be than the fat weed
That roots itself in ease on Lethe wharf,
Wouldst thou not stir in this. Now, Hamlet, hear:
'Tis given out that, sleeping in my orchard,
A serpent stung me; so the whole ear of Denmark

Is by a forged process of my death
Rankly abused: but know, thou noble youth,
The serpent that did sting thy father's life
Now wears his crown.

HAMLET: O my prophetic soul! My uncle!

GHOST: Ay, that incestuous, that adulterate beast,
With witchcraft of his wit, with traitorous gifts,
O wicked wit and gifts, that have the power
So to seduce! won to his shameful lust
The will of my most seeming-virtuous queen:
O Hamlet, what a falling-off was there!
From me, whose love was of that dignity
That it went hand in hand, even with the vow
I made to her in marriage, and to decline
Upon a wretch whose natural gifts were poor
To those of mine!
But virtue, as it never will be moved,
Though lewdness court it in a shape of heaven,
So lust, though to a radiant angel link'd,
Will sate itself in a celestial bed,
And prey on garbage.
But, soft! methinks I scent the morning air;
Brief let me be. Sleeping within my orchard,
My custom always of the afternoon,
Upon my secure hour thy uncle stole,
With juice of cursed hebenon in a vial,

And in the porches of my ears did pour
The leperous distilment; whose effect
Holds such an enmity with blood of man,
That swift as quicksilver it courses through
The natural gates and alleys of the body,
And with a sudden vigour doth posset
And curd, like eager droppings into milk,
The thin and wholesome blood: so did it mine;
And a most instant tetter bak'd about,
Most lazar-like, with vile and loathsome crust,
All my smooth body.
Thus was I, sleeping, by a brother's hand
Of life, of crown, of queen, at once dispatch'd:
Cut off even in the blossoms of my sin,
Unhousel'd, disappointed, unanel'd,
No reckoning made, but sent to my account
With all my imperfections on my head:
O, horrible! O, horrible! most horrible!
If thou hast nature in thee, bear it not;
Let not the royal bed of Denmark be
A couch for luxury and damned incest.
But, howsoever thou pursuest this act,
Taint not thy mind, nor let thy soul contrive
Against thy mother aught: leave her to heaven,
And to those thorns that in her bosom lodge,
To prick and sting her. Fare thee well at once!

The glow-worm shows the matin to be near,
And 'gins to pale his uneffectual fire:
Adieu, adieu! Hamlet, remember me.

Exeunt

HAMLET: O all you host of heaven! O earth! what else?
And shall I couple hell? O, fie! Hold, hold, my heart;
And you, my sinews, grow not instant old,
But bear me stiffly up. Remember thee!
Ay, thou poor ghost, while memory holds a seat
In this distracted globe. Remember thee!
Yea, from the table of my memory,
I'll wipe away all trivial fond records,
All saws of books, all forms, all pressures past,
That youth and observation copied there;
And thy commandment all alone shall live
Within the book and volume of my brain,
Unmix'd with baser matter: yes, yes, by heaven!
O most pernicious woman!
O villain, villain, smiling, damned villain!
My tables, meet it is I set it down,
That one may smile, and smile, and be a villain;
At least I'm sure it may be so in Denmark:
So, uncle, there you are. Now to my word;
It is 'Adieu, adieu! remember me.'
I have sworn 't.

MARCELLUS: }
HORATIO: } *Within.* My lord, my lord,

MARCELLUS: Lord Hamlet.

HORATIO: Heaven secure him!

HAMLET: So be it!

HORATIO: Hillo, ho, ho, my Lord!

HAMLET: Hillo, ho, ho, boy! come, bird, come.

Enter Horatio and Marcellus

MARCELLUS: How is't, my noble Lord?

HORATIO: What news, my Lord?

HAMLET: O, wonderful!

HORATIO: Good my Lord, tell it.

HAMLET: No; you'll reveal it.

HORATIO: Not I, my Lord, by heaven.

MARCELLUS: Nor I, my Lord.

HAMLET: How say you, then; would heart of man once think it?
But you'll be secret?

BOTH: Ay, by heaven, my Lord.

HAMLET: There's ne'er a villain dwelling in all Denmark
But he's an arrant knave.

HORATIO: There needs no ghost, my Lord, come from the grave
To tell us this.

HAMLET: Why, right; you are i' th' right;
And so, without more circumstance at all,

I hold it fit that we shake hands and part:
You, as your business and desire shall point you;
For every man has business and desire,
Such as it is; and for mine own poor part,
Look you, I'll go pray.

HORATIO: These are but wild and whirling words, my Lord.

HAMLET: I'm sorry they offend you, heartily;
Yes, 'faith heartily.

HORATIO: There's no offence, my Lord.

HAMLET: Yes, by Saint Patrick, but there is, Horatio,
And much offence too. Touching this vision here,
It is an honest ghost, that let me tell you:
For your desire to know what is between us,
O'ermaster 't as you may. And now, good friends,
As you are friends, scholars and soldiers,
Give me one poor request.

HORATIO: What is't, my Lord? We will.

HAMLET: Never make known what you have seen to-night.

BOTH: My Lord, we will not.

HAMLET: Nay, but swear't.

HORATIO: In faith,
My Lord, not I.

MARCELLUS: Nor I, my Lord, in faith.

HAMLET: Upon my sword.

MARCELLUS: We have sworn, my Lord, already.

HAMLET: Indeed, upon my sword, indeed.

Ghost cries under the stage.

GHOST: Swear.

HAMLET: Ah, ha, boy! say'st thou so? Art thou there, truepenny?
Come on you hear this fellow in the cellarage
Consent to swear.

HORATIO: Propose the oath, my Lord.

HAMLET: Never to speak of this that you have seen,
Swear by my sword.

GHOST: Swear.

HAMLET: *Hic et ubique?* Then we'll shift our ground.
Come hither, gentlemen,
And lay your hands again upon my sword:
Never to speak of this that you have heard,
Swear by my sword.

GHOST: Swear.

HAMLET: Well said, old mole! canst work i' th' ground so fast?
A worthy pioner! Once more remove, good friends.

HORATIO: O day and night, but this is wondrous strange!

HAMLET: And therefore as a stranger give it welcome.
There are more things in heaven and earth, Horatio,
Than are dreamt of in your philosophy. But come;
Here, as before, never, so help you mercy,
How strange or odd soe'er I bear myself,

As I perchance hereafter shall think meet
To put an antic disposition on,
That you, at such times seeing me, never shall,
With arms encumber'd thus, or this headshake,
Or by pronouncing of some doubtful phrase,
As 'Well, well, we know,' or 'We could, and if we would,'
Or 'If we list to speak,' or 'There be, an if they might,'
Or such ambiguous giving out, to note
That you know aught of me: this not to do,
So grace and mercy at your most need help you, Swear.

GHOST: Swear.

HAMLET: Rest, rest, perturbed spirit!

They swear

So, gentlemen,
With all my love I do commend me to you:
And what so poor a man as Hamlet is
May do, to express his love and friending to you,
God willing, shall not lack. Let us go in together;
And still your fingers on your lips, I pray.
The time is out of joint: O cursed spite,
That ever I was born to set it right!
Nay, come, let's go together.

Exeunt

II. 1

Enter Polonius and Reynaldo

POLONIUS: Give him this money and these notes, Reynaldo.

REYNALDO: I will, my Lord.

POLONIUS: You shall do marvellous wisely, good Reynaldo,
Before you visit him, to make inquire
Of his behaviour.

REYNALDO: My Lord, I did intend it.

POLONIUS: Marry, well said; very well said. Look you, sir,
Inquire me first what Danskers are in Paris;
And how, and who, what means, and where they keep,
What company, at what expense; and finding
By this encompassment and drift of question,
That they do know my son, come you more nearer
Than your particular demands will touch it:
Take you, as 'twere, some distant knowledge of him;
As thus, 'I know his father and his friends,
And in part him:' do you mark this, Reynaldo?

REYNALDO: Ay, very well, my Lord.

POLONIUS: And in part him; but you may say 'not well'
But, if't be he I mean, he's very wild;
Addicted so and so: and there put on him
What forgeries you please; marry, none so rank
As may dishonour him; take heed of that;

But, sir, such wanton, wild and usual slips
As are companions noted and most known
To youth and liberty.

REYNALDO: As gaming, my Lord.

POLONIUS: Ay, or drinking, fencing, swearing, quarrelling,
Drabbing: you may go so far.

REYNALDO: My Lord, that would dishonour him.

POLONIUS: 'Faith, no; as you may season it in the charge
You must not put another scandal on him,
That he is open to incontinency;
That's not my meaning: but breathe his faults so quaintly
That they may seem the taints of liberty,
The flash and outbreak of a fiery mind,
A savageness in unreclaimed blood,
Of general assault.

REYNALDO: But, my good Lord–

POLONIUS: Wherefore should you do this?

REYNALDO: Ay, my Lord,
I would know that.

POLONIUS: Marry, sir, here's my drift;
And I believe, it is a fetch of wit:
You laying these slight sullies on my son,
As 'twere a thing a little soil'd i' th' working, Mark you,
Your party in converse, him you would sound,
Having ever seen in the prenominate crimes

The youth you breathe of guilty, be assured
He closes with you in this consequence;
'Good sir,' or so, or 'friend,' or 'gentleman,'
According to the phrase or the addition
Of man and country.

REYNALDO: Very good, my Lord.

POLONIUS: And then, sir, does he this, he does: what was I about to say? By the mass, I was about to say something: where did I leave?

REYNALDO: At 'closes in the consequence,' at 'friend or so,' and 'gentleman.'

POLONIUS: At 'closes in the consequence,' ay, marry;
He closes thus: 'I know the gentleman;
I saw him yesterday, or t' other day,
Or then, or then; with such, or such; and, as you say,
There was a' gaming; there o'ertook in's rouse;
There falling out at tennis: or perchance,
'I saw him enter such a house of sale,'
Videlicet, a brothel, or so forth.
See you now;
Your bait of falsehood takes this carp of truth:
And thus do we of wisdom and of reach,
With windlasses and with assays of bias,
By indirections find directions out:
So by my former lecture and advice,
Shall you my son. You have me, have you not?

REYNALDO: My Lord, I have.
POLONIUS: God be wi' you; fare you well.
REYNALDO: Good my Lord!
POLONIUS: Observe his inclination in yourself.
REYNALDO: I shall, my Lord.
POLONIUS: And let him ply his music.
REYNALDO: Well, my Lord.
POLONIUS: Farewell!

Exit Reynaldo

Enter Ophelia

How now, Ophelia! what's the matter?
OPHELIA: O, my Lord, my Lord, I have been so affrighted!
POLONIUS: With what, i' th' name of God?
OPHELIA: My Lord, as I was sewing in my closet,
Lord Hamlet, with his doublet all unbraced;
No hat upon his head; his stockings foul'd,
Ungarter'd, and down-gyved to his ankle;
Pale as his shirt; his knees knocking each other;
And with a look so piteous in purport
As if he had been loosed out of hell,
To speak of horrors, he comes before me.
POLONIUS: Mad for thy love?
OPHELIA: My Lord, I do not know;
But truly, I do fear it.
POLONIUS: What said he?
OPHELIA: He took me by the wrist and held me hard;

Then goes he to the length of all his arm;
And, with his other hand thus o'er his brow,
He falls to such perusal of my face
As he would draw it. Long stay'd he so;
At last, a little shaking of mine arm:
And thrice his head thus waving up and down,
He raised a sigh so piteous and profound,
As it did seem to shatter all his bulk
And end his being: that done, he lets me go:
And, with his head over his shoulder turn'd,
He seem'd to find his way without his eyes;
For out o' doors he went without their help,
And, to the last, bended their light on me.

POLONIUS: Come, go with me: I will go seek the King.
This is the very ecstasy of love,
Whose violent property fordoes itself
And leads the will to desperate undertakings
As oft as any passion under heaven
That does afflict our natures. I am sorry.
What, have you given him any hard words of late?

OPHELIA: No, my good Lord, but, as you did command,
I did repel his fetters and denied
His access to me.

POLONIUS: That hath made him mad.
I am sorry that with better heed and judgment
I had not quoted him: I fear'd he did but trifle,

And meant to wreck thee; but, beshrew my jealousy!
It seems, it is as proper to our age
To cast beyond ourselves in our opinions
As it is common for the younger sort
To lack discretion. Come, go we to the King:
This must be known; which, being kept close, might move
More grief to hide than hate to utter love.

Exeunt

II. 2

Enter King Claudius, Queen Gertrude, Rosencrantz, Guildenstern, and Attendants

KING: Welcome, dear Rosencrantz and Guildenstern!
Moreover that we much did long to see you,
The need we have to use you, did provoke
Our hasty sending. Something have you heard
Of Hamlet's transformation; so call it,
Sith nor the exterior nor the inward man
Resembles that it was. What it should be,
More than his father's death, that thus hath put him
So much from the understanding of himself,
I cannot dream of: I entreat you both,
That, being of so young days brought up with him,
And sith so neighbour'd to his youth and humour,
That you vouchsafe your rest here in our Court

Some little time: so by your companies
To draw him on to pleasures, and to gather,
So much as from occasion you may glean,
Whether aught, to us unknown, afflicts him thus,
That, open'd, lies within our remedy.

QUEEN: Good gentlemen, he hath much talk'd of you;
And sure I am, two men there are not living
To whom he more adheres. If it will please you
To show us so much gentry and goodwill
As to expend your time with us awhile,
For the supply and profit of our hope,
Your visitation shall receive such thanks
As fits a King's remembrance.

ROSENCRANTZ: Both your Majesties
Might, by the sovereign power you have of us,
Put your dread pleasures more into command
Than to entreaty.

GUILDENSTERN: We both obey,
And here give up ourselves, in the full bent
To lay our service freely at your feet,
To be commanded.

KING: Thanks, Rosencrantz and gentle Guildenstern.

QUEEN: Thanks, Guildenstern and gentle Rosencrantz:
And I beseech you instantly to visit
My too much changed son. Go, some of you,
And bring these gentlemen where Hamlet is.

GUILDENSTERN: Heavens make our presence and our practises
Pleasant and helpful to him!

Exeunt with others.

QUEEN: Ay, amen!

Enter Polonius

POLONIUS: The ambassadors from Norway, my good Lord,
Are joyfully return'd.

KING: Thou still hast been the father of good news.

POLONIUS: Have I, my Lord? I assure my good Liege,
I hold my duty, as I hold my soul,
Both to my God and to my gracious King:
And I do think, or else this brain of mine
Hunts not the trail of policy, so sure
As it hath used to do, that I have found
The very cause of Hamlet's lunacy.

KING: O, speak of that; that do I long to hear.

POLONIUS: Give first admittance to th' ambassadors;
My news shall be the fruit to that great feast.

KING: Thyself do grace to them, and bring them in.

Exit Polonius

He tells me, my dear Gertrude, he hath found
The head and source of all your son's distemper.

QUEEN: I doubt it is no other but the main;
His father's death, and our o'erhasty marriage.

KING: Well, we shall sift him.

Enter Polonius, with Voltemand and Cornelius

Welcome, my good friends!
Say, Voltemand, what from our brother Norway?

VOLTEMAND: Most fair return of greetings and desires.
Upon our first, he sent out to suppress
His nephew's levies; which to him appear'd
To be a preparation 'gainst the Polack;
But, better look'd into, he truly found
It was against your Highness: whereat grieved,
That so his sickness, age and impotence
Was falsely borne in hand, sends out arrests
On Fortinbras; which he, in brief, obeys;
Receives rebuke from Norway, and in fine
Makes vow before his uncle, never more
To give th' assay of arms against your Majesty.
Whereon old Norway, overcome with joy,
Gives him three thousand crowns in annual fee,
And his commission to employ those soldiers,
So levied as before, against the Polack:
With an entreaty, herein further shown,
That it might please you to give quiet pass
Through your dominions for this enterprise,
On such regards of safety and allowance
As therein are set down.

KING: It likes us well;

And at our more consider'd time, we'll, read,
Answer, and think upon this business.
Meantime we thank you for your well-took labour:
Go to your rest; at night we'll feast together:
Most welcome home!

Exeunt Voltemand and Cornelius

POLONIUS: This business is well ended.
My Liege, and Madam, to expostulate
What Majesty should be, what duty is,
Why day is day, night night, and time is time,
Were nothing but to waste night, day and time.
Therefore, since brevity is the soul of wit,
And tediousness the limbs and outward flourishes,
I will be brief: your noble son is mad:
Mad call I it; for, to define true, madness,
What is't but to be nothing else but mad?
But let that go.

QUEEN: More matter, with less art.

POLONIUS: Madam, I swear I use no art at all.
That he is mad, 'tis true: 'tis true 'tis pity;
And pity 'tis true: a foolish figure;
But farewell it, for I will use no art.
Mad let us grant him, then: and now remains
That we find out the cause of this effect,
Or rather say, the cause of this defect,
For this effect defective comes by cause:

Thus it remains, and the remainder thus. Perpend.
I have a daughter; have, while she is mine
Who, in her duty and obedience, mark,
Hath given me this: now gather, and surmise.
[Reads] 'To the celestial and my soul's idol, the most beautified Ophelia,'
That's an ill phrase, a vile phrase; 'beautified' is a vile phrase: but you shall hear. Thus:
[Reads] 'In her excellent white bosom, these, &c.'

QUEEN: Came this from Hamlet to her?

POLONIUS: Good Madam, stay awhile; I will be faithful.
[Reads] 'Doubt thou the stars are fire;
Doubt that the sun doth move;
Doubt truth to be a liar;
But never doubt, I love.
'O dear Ophelia, I am ill at these numbers;
I have not art to reckon my groans: but that
I love thee best, O most best, believe it. Adieu.
'Thine evermore most dear lady, whilst
this machine is to him.' Hamlet.
This, in obedience, hath my daughter shown me,
And more above, hath his solicitings,
As they fell out by time, by means and place,
All given to mine ear.

KING: But how hath she received his love?

POLONIUS: What do you think of me?

KING: As of a man, faithful and honourable.

POLONIUS: I would fain prove so. But what might you think,
When I had seen this hot love on the wing
As I perceived it, I must tell you that,
Before my daughter told me what might you,
Or my dear Majesty your Queen here, think,
If I had play'd the desk or table-book,
Or given my heart a winking, mute and dumb,
Or look'd upon this love with idle sight;
What might you think? No, I went round to work,
And my young mistress thus I did bespeak:
'Lord Hamlet is a prince, out of thy star;
This must not be:' and then I precepts gave her,
That she should lock herself from his resort,
Admit no messengers, receive no tokens.
Which done, she took the fruits of my advice;
And he, repulsed a short tale to make,
Fell into a sadness, then into a fast,
Thence to a watch, thence into a weakness,
Thence to a lightness, and, by this declension,
Into the madness wherein now he raves,
And all we mourn for.

KING: Do you think 'tis this?

QUEEN: It may be, very likely.

POLONIUS: Hath there been such a time I'd fain know that

That I have positively said 'Tis so,
When it proved otherwise?

KING: Not that I know.

POLONIUS: Take this from this, if this be otherwise:
If circumstances lead me, I will find
Where truth is hid, though it were hid indeed
Within the centre.

KING: How may we try it further?

POLONIUS: You know, sometimes he walks four hours together
Here in the lobby.

QUEEN: So he does indeed.

POLONIUS: At such a time I'll loose my daughter to him:
Be you and I behind an arras then;
Mark the encounter: if he love her not,
And be not from his reason fall'n thereon,
Let me be no assistant for a state,
But keep a farm and carters.

KING: We will try it.

Enter Hamlet, reading a book

QUEEN: But, look, where sadly the poor wretch comes reading.

POLONIUS: Away, I do beseech you, both away:
I'll board him presently.

Exeunt King and Queen

O, give me leave:
How does my good Lord Hamlet?

HAMLET: Well, God-a-mercy.

POLONIUS: Do you know me, my Lord?

HAMLET: Excellent well; you are a fishmonger.

POLONIUS: Not I, my Lord.

HAMLET: Then I would you were so honest a man.

POLONIUS: Honest, my Lord!

HAMLET: Ay, sir; to be honest, as this world goes, is to be one man picked out of ten thousand.

POLONIUS: That's very true, my Lord.

HAMLET: For if the sun breed maggots in a dead dog, being a god kissing carrion, have you a daughter?

POLONIUS: I have, my Lord.

HAMLET: Let her not walk i' th' sun: conception is a blessing: but not as your daughter may conceive. Friend, look to 't.

POLONIUS: How say you by that? Still harping on my daughter: yet he knew me not at first; he said I was a fishmonger: he is far gone, far gone: and truly in my youth I suffered much extremity for love; very near this. I'll speak to him again. What do you read, my Lord?

HAMLET: Words, words, words.

POLONIUS: What is the matter, my Lord?

HAMLET: Between who?

POLONIUS: I mean, the matter that you read, my Lord.

HAMLET: Slanders, sir: for the satirical rogue says here that old men have grey beards, that their faces are wrinkled, their eyes purging thick amber or plum-tree gum and that they have a plentiful lack of wit, together with most weak hams: all which, sir, though I most powerfully and potently believe, yet I hold it not honesty to have it thus set down, for yourself, sir, should be old as I am, if like a crab you could go backward.

POLONIUS: Though this be madness, yet there is method in 't. Will you walk out of the air, my Lord?

HAMLET: Into my grave.

POLONIUS: Indeed, that is out o' th' air.

How pregnant sometimes his replies are! a happiness that often madness hits on, which reason and sanity could not so prosperously be delivered of. I will leave him, and suddenly contrive the means of meeting between him and my daughter.—My honourable Lord, I will most humbly take my leave of you.

HAMLET: You cannot, sir, take from me any thing that I will more willingly part withal: except my life, except my life, except my life.

POLONIUS: Fare you well, my Lord.

HAMLET: These tedious old fools!

Enter Rosencrantz and Guildenstern

POLONIUS: You go to seek my Lord Hamlet; there he is.

ROSENCRANTZ: [To Polonius] God save you, sir!

Exit Polonius

GUILDENSTERN: My honoured Lord!

ROSENCRANTZ: My most dear Lord!

HAMLET: My excellent good friends! How dost thou, Guildenstern? Ah, Rosencrantz! Good lads, how do ye both?

ROSENCRANTZ: As the indifferent children of the earth.

GUILDENSTERN: Happy, in that we are not over-happy; On fortune's cap we are not the very button.

HAMLET: Nor the soles of her shoe?

ROSENCRANTZ: Neither, my Lord.

HAMLET: Then you live about her waist, or in the middle of her favours?

GUILDENSTERN: Faith, her privates, we.

HAMLET: In the secret parts of fortune? O, most true; she is a strumpet. What's the news?

ROSENCRANTZ: None, my Lord, but that the world's grown honest.

HAMLET: Then is Doomsday near: but your news is not true. Let me question more in particular: what have you, my good friends, deserved at the hands of fortune, that she sends you to prison hither?

GUILDENSTERN: Prison, my Lord?

HAMLET: Denmark's a prison.

ROSENCRANTZ: Then is the world one.

HAMLET: A goodly one; in which there are many confines, wards and dungeons, Denmark being one o' the worst.

ROSENCRANTZ: We think not so, my Lord.

HAMLET: Why, then, 'tis none to you; for there is nothing either good or bad, but thinking makes it so: to me it is a prison.

ROSENCRANTZ: Why then, your ambition makes it one; 'tis too narrow for your mind.

HAMLET: O God, I could be bounded in a nut-shell and count myself a king of infinite space, were it not that I have bad dreams.

GUILDENSTERN: Which dreams indeed are ambition, for the very substance of the ambitions is merely the shadow of a dream.

HAMLET: A dream itself is but a shadow.

ROSENCRANTZ: Truly, and I hold ambition of so airy and light a quality that it is but a shadow's shadow.

HAMLET: Then are our beggars bodies, and our monarchs and outstretched heroes the beggars' shadows. Shall we to the Court: for, by my fay, I cannot reason.

BOTH: We'll wait upon you.

HAMLET: No such matter: I will not sort you with the rest of my servants, for, to speak to you like an honest man, I am most dreadfully attended. But, in the beaten way of friendship, what make you at Elsinore?

ROSENCRANTZ: To visit you, my Lord; on other occasion.

HAMLET: Beggar that I am, I am even poor in thanks;

but I thank you: and sure, dear friends, my thanks are too dear a halfpenny. Were you not sent for? Is it your own inclining? Is it a free visitation? Come, deal justly with me: come, come; nay, speak.

GUILDENSTERN: What should we say, my Lord?

HAMLET: Why, any thing, but to the purpose. You were sent for; and there is a kind of confession in your looks which your modesties have not craft enough to colour: I know the good King and Queen have sent for you.

ROSENCRANTZ: To what end, my Lord?

HAMLET: That you must teach me. But let me conjure you, by the rights of our fellowship, by the consonancy of our youth, by the obligation of our ever-preserved love, and by what more dear a better proposer could charge you withal, be even and direct with me, whether you were sent for, or no?

ROSENCRANTZ: [Aside to Guildenstern] What say you?

HAMLET: [Aside] Nay, then, I have an eye of you.—If you love me, hold not off.

GUILDENSTERN: My Lord, we were sent for.

HAMLET: I will tell you why; so shall my anticipation prevent your discovery, and your secrecy to the King and Queen moult no feather. I have of late—but wherefore I know not—lost all my mirth, forgone all custom of exercises; and indeed it goes so heavily with my disposition that this goodly frame, the earth, seems to me a sterile promontory, this most excellent canopy, the air, look you, this brave o'erhanging firmament, this majestical roof fretted with golden fire, why, it appears no other thing to me than a foul and pestilent congregation of vapours. What a piece of work is a man! how noble in reason! how infinite in faculty! in form and moving how express and admirable! in action, how like an angel! in apprehension, how like a god! the beauty of the world! the paragon of animals! And yet, to me, what is this quintessence of dust? man delights not me: no, nor woman neither, though by your smiling you seem to say so.

ROSENCRANTZ: My Lord, there was no such stuff in my thoughts.

HAMLET: Why did you laugh then, when I said 'man delights not me'?

ROSENCRANTZ: To think, my Lord, if you delight not in man, what lenten entertainment the players shall receive from you: we coted them on the way; and hither are they coming, to offer you service.

HAMLET: He that plays the king shall be welcome; his majesty shall have tribute of me; the adventurous knight shall use his foil and target; the lover shall not sigh *gratis;* the humorous man shall end his part in peace; the clown shall make those laugh whose lungs are tickled o' the sere; and the lady shall say her mind freely, or the blank verse shall halt for't. What players are they?

ROSENCRANTZ: Even those you were wont to take delight in, the tragedians of the city.

HAMLET: How chances it they travel? Their residence, both in reputation and profit, was better both ways.

ROSENCRANTZ: I think their inhibition comes by the means of the late innovation.

HAMLET: Do they hold the same estimation they did when I was in the city? Are they so followed?

ROSENCRANTZ: No, indeed, they are not.

HAMLET: How comes it? Do they grow rusty?

ROSENCRANTZ: Nay, their endeavour keeps in the wonted pace: but there is, sir, an aery of children, little eyases, that cry out on the top of question, and are most tyrannically clapped for't: these are now the fashion, and so berattle the common stages—so they call them—that many wearing rapiers are afraid of goose-quills and dare scarce come thither.

HAMLET: What, are they children? Who maintains 'em? How are they escoted? Will they pursue the quality no longer than they can sing? Will they not say afterwards, if they should grow themselves to common players—as it is most like, if their means are no better—their writers do them wrong, to make them exclaim against their own succession?

ROSENCRANTZ: 'Faith, there has been much to do on both sides; and the nation holds it no sin, to tarre them to controversy: there was, for a while, no money bid for argument, unless the poet and the player went to cuffs in the question.

HAMLET: Is't possible?

GUILDENSTERN: O, there has been much throwing about of brains.

HAMLET: Do the boys carry it away?

ROSENCRANTZ: Ay, that they do, my Lord; Hercules and his load too.

HAMLET: It is not very strange; for mine uncle is King of Denmark, and those that would make mows at him while my father lived, give twenty, forty, fifty, an hundred ducats a-piece for his picture in little. 'Sblood, there is something in this more than natural, if philosophy could find it out.

Flourish of trumpets within

GUILDENSTERN: There are the players.

HAMLET: Gentlemen, you are welcome to Elsinore. Your hands, come then: the appurtenance of welcome is fashion and ceremony: let me comply with you in this garb, lest my extent to the players, which, I tell you, must show fairly outward, should more appear like entertainment than yours. You are welcome: but my uncle-father and aunt-mother are deceived.

GUILDENSTERN: In what, my dear Lord?

HAMLET: I am but mad north-north-west: when the wind is southerly I know a hawk from a handsaw.

Enter Polonius

POLONIUS: Well be with you, gentlemen!

HAMLET: Hark you, Guildenstern; and you too: at each ear a hearer: that great baby you see there is not yet out of his swaddling-clouts.

ROSENCRANTZ: Happily he's the second time come to them; for they say an old man is twice a child.

HAMLET: I will prophesy, he comes to tell me of the players; mark it. You say right, sir: for a' Monday morning; 'twas so indeed.

POLONIUS: My Lord, I have news to tell you.

HAMLET: My Lord, I have news to tell you. When Roscius was an actor in Rome.

POLONIUS: The actors are come hither, my Lord.

HAMLET: Buz, buz!

POLONIUS: Upon mine honour.

HAMLET: Then came each actor on his ass.

POLONIUS: The best actors in the world, either for tragedy, comedy, history, pastoral, pastoral-comical, historical-pastoral, tragical-historical, tragical- comical-historical-pastoral, scene individable, or poem unlimited: Seneca cannot be too heavy, nor Plautus too light. For the law of writ and the liberty, these are the only men.

HAMLET: O Jephthah, judge of Israel, what a treasure hadst thou!

POLONIUS: What a treasure had he, my Lord?

HAMLET: Why,

'One fair daughter and no more,
The which he loved passing well.'

POLONIUS: [Aside] Still on my daughter.

HAMLET: Am I not i' th' right, old Jephthah?

POLONIUS: If you call me Jephthah, my Lord, I have a daughter that I love passing well.

HAMLET: Nay, that follows not.

POLONIUS: What follows, then, my Lord?

HAMLET: Why, 'As by lot, God wot,' and then, you know, 'It came to pass, as most like it was,'— the first row of the pious chanson will show you more; for look, where my abridgement comes.

Enter four or five Players

You are welcome, masters; welcome, all. I am glad to see thee well. Welcome, good friends. O, my old friend! thy face is valanced since I saw thee last: comest thou to beard me in Denmark? What, my young lady and mistress! By'r lady, your ladyship is nearer to heaven than when I saw you last, by the altitude of a chopine. Pray God, your voice, like apiece of uncurrent gold, be not cracked within the ring. Masters, you are all welcome. We'll e'en to't like French falconers, fly at any thing we see: we'll have a speech straight: come, give us a taste of your quality; come, a passionate speech.

FIRST PLAYER: What speech, my Lord?

HAMLET: I heard thee speak me a speech once, but it was never acted; or, if it was, not above once; for the play, I remember, pleased not the million; 'twas caviare to the general: but it was—as I received it, and others, whose judgments in such matters cried in the top of mine—an excellent play, well digested in the scenes, set down with as much modesty as cunning. I remember, one said there were no sallets in the lines to make the matter savoury, nor no matter in the phrase that might indict the author of affectation; but called it an honest method, as wholesome as sweet, and by very much more handsome than fine. One speech in it I chiefly loved: 'twas Aeneas' tale to Dido; and thereabout of it especially, where he speaks of Priam's slaughter: if it live in your memory, begin at this line: let me see, let me see—

'The rugged Pyrrhus, like the Hyrcanian beast,'—
It is not so:—it begins with Pyrrhus:
'The rugged Pyrrhus, he whose sable arms,
Black as his purpose, did the night resemble
When he lay couched in the ominous horse,
Hath now this dread and black complexion smear'd
With heraldry more dismal; head to foot
Now is he total gules; horridly trick'd
With blood of fathers, mothers, daughters, sons,
Baked and impasted with the parching streets,
That lend a tyrannous and damned light
To their vile murders: roasted in wrath and fire,
And thus o'er-sized with coagulate gore,
With eyes like carbuncles, the hellish Pyrrhus
Old grandsire Priam seeks.'

So, proceed you.

POLONIUS: 'Fore God, my Lord, well spoken, with good accent and good discretion.

FIRST PLAYER: 'Anon he finds him
Striking too short at Greeks; his antique sword,
Rebellious to his arm, lies where it falls,
Repugnant to command: unequal match'd,
Pyrrhus at Priam drives; in rage strikes wide;
But with the whiff and wind of his fell sword
The unnerved father falls. Then senseless Ilium,
Seeming to feel this blow, with flaming top
Stoops to his base, and with a hideous crash
Takes prisoner Pyrrhus' ear: for, lo! his sword,
Which was declining on the milky head
Of reverend Priam, seem'd i' the air to stick:
So, as a painted tyrant, Pyrrhus stood,
And like a neutral to his will and matter,
Did nothing.
But, as we often see, against some storm,
A silence in the heavens, the rack stand still,
The bold winds speechless and the orb below
As hush as death, anon the dreadful thunder
Doth rend the region, so, after Pyrrhus' pause,
Aroused vengeance sets him new a-work;
And never did the Cyclops' hammers fall
On Mars's armour forged for proof eterne
With less remorse than Pyrrhus' bleeding sword

Now falls on Priam.
Out, out, thou strumpet, Fortune! All you gods,
In general Synod 'take away her power;
Break all the spokes and fellies from her wheel,
And bowl the round nave down the hill of heaven,
As low as to the fiends!'

POLONIUS: This is too long.

HAMLET: It shall to th' barber's, with your beard. Prithee, say on: he's for a jig or a tale of bawdry, or he sleeps: say on: come to Hecuba.

FIRST PLAYER: 'But who, O who, had seen the mobled Queen—'

HAMLET: 'The mobled Queen?'

POLONIUS: That's good; 'mobled queen' is good.

FIRST PLAYER: 'Run barefoot up and down, threatening the flames
With bisson rheum; a clout upon that head
Where late the diadem stood, and for a robe,
About her lank and all o'er-teemed loins,
A blanket, in the alarm of fear caught up;
Who this had seen, with tongue in venom steep'd,
'Gainst Fortune's state would treason have pronounced:
But if the gods themselves did see her then,
When she saw Pyrrhus make malicious sport
In mincing with his sword her husband's limbs,
The instant burst of clamour that she made,

Unless things mortal move them not at all,
Would have made milch the burning eyes of heaven,
And passion in the gods.'

POLONIUS: Look, whether he has not turned his colour and has tears in's eyes. Pray you, no more.

HAMLET: 'Tis well: I'll have thee speak out the rest soon. Good my lord, will you see the players well bestowed? Do you hear, let them be well used; for they are the abstract and brief chronicles of the time: after your death you were better have a bad epitaph than their ill report while you live.

POLONIUS: My Lord, I will use them according to their desert.

HAMLET: God's bodykins, man, much better: use every man after his desert, and who should 'scape whipping? Use them after your own honour and dignity: the less they deserve, the more merit is in your bounty. Take them in.

POLONIUS: Come, sirs.

HAMLET: Follow him, friends: we'll hear a play to-morrow.

Exit Polonius with all the Players but the First

Dost thou hear me, old friend; can you play the Murder of Gonzago?

FIRST PLAYER: Ay, my Lord.

HAMLET: We'll ha't to-morrow night. You could, for a need, study a speech of some dozen or sixteen lines, which I would set down and insert in't, could you not?

FIRST PLAYER: Ay, my Lord.

HAMLET: Very well. Follow that Lord; and look you mock him not.

My good friends, I'll leave you till night: you are welcome to Elsinore.

ROSENCRANTZ: Good my Lord!

HAMLET: Ay, so, God be wi' ye;

Exeunt Rosencrantz and Guildenstern

Now I am alone.
O, what a rogue and peasant slave am I!
Is it not monstrous that this player here,
But in a fiction, in a dream of passion,
Could force his soul so to his own conceit,
That from her working all his visage wann'd,
Tears in his eyes, distraction in's aspect,
A broken voice, and his whole function suiting
With forms to his conceit? And all for nothing!
For Hecuba!
What's Hecuba to him, or he to Hecuba,
That he should weep for her? What would he do,
Had he the motive and the cue for passion
That I have? He would drown the stage with tears
And cleave the general ear with horrid speech,
Make mad the guilty and appal the free,
Confound the ignorant, and amaze indeed
The very faculties of eyes and ears. Yet I,

A dull and muddy-mettled rascal, peak,
Like John-a-dreams, unpregnant of my cause,
And can say nothing; no, not for a king,
Upon whose property and most dear life,
A damn'd defeat was made. Am I a coward?
Who calls me villain? breaks my pate across?
Plucks off my beard, and blows it in my face?
Tweaks me by the nose? gives me the lie i' the throat,
As deep as to the lungs? who does me this?
Ha! Why I should take it: for it cannot be
But I am pigeon-liver'd and lack gall
To make oppression bitter, or ere this,
I should have fatted all the region kites
With this slave's offal: bloody, bawdy villain!
Remorseless, treacherous, lecherous, kindless villain!
O, vengeance!
Why, what an ass am I! This is most brave,
That I, the son of a dear father murder'd,
Prompted to my revenge by heaven and hell,
Must, like a whore, unpack my heart with words,
And fall a-cursing, like a very drab,
A scullion!
Fie upon't! foh! About, my brain! I have heard
That guilty creatures sitting at a play
Have by the very cunning of the scene,
Been struck so to the soul that presently

They have proclaim'd their malefactions;
For murder, though it have no tongue, will speak
With most miraculous organ. I'll have these players,
Play something like the murder of my father
Before mine uncle: I'll observe his looks;
I'll tent him to the quick: if he but blench,
I know my course. The spirit that I have seen
May be the devil: and the devil hath power
To assume a pleasing shape; yea, and perhaps
Out of my weakness and my melancholy,
As he is very potent with such spirits,
Abuses me to damn me: I'll have grounds
More relative than this: the play's the thing
Wherein I'll catch the conscience of the King.

Exit

III. 1

Enter King Claudius, Queen Gertrude, Polonius, Ophelia, Rosencrantz, and Guildenstern

KING: And can you, by no drift of circumstance,
Get from him why he puts on this confusion,
Grating so harshly all his days of quiet
With turbulent and dangerous lunacy?

ROSENCRANTZ: He does confess he feels himself distracted;
But from what cause he will by no means speak.

GUILDENSTERN: Nor do we find him forward to be sounded,
But, with a crafty madness, keeps aloof,
When we would bring him on to some confession
Of his true state.
QUEEN: Did he receive you well?
ROSENCRANTZ: Most like a gentleman.
GUILDENSTERN: But with much forcing of his disposition.
ROSENCRANTZ: Niggard of question; but, of our demands,
Most free in his reply.
QUEEN: Did you assay him?
To any pastime?
ROSENCRANTZ: Madam, it so fell out, that certain players
We o'er-raught on the way: of these we told him;
And there did seem in him a kind of joy
To hear of it: they are about the Court,
And, as I think, they have already order
This night to play before him.
POLONIUS: 'Tis most true:
And he beseech'd me to entreat your Majesties
To hear and see the matter.
KING: With all my heart; and it doth much content me
To hear him so inclined.
Good gentlemen, give him a further edge,
And drive his purpose on to these delights.

ROSENCRANTZ: We shall, my Lord.

Exeunt Rosencrantz and Guildenstern

KING: Sweet Gertrude, leave us too;
For we have closely sent for Hamlet hither,
That he, as 'twere by accident, may here
Affront Ophelia:
Her father and myself, lawful espials,
Will so bestow ourselves that, seeing, unseen,
We may of their encounter frankly judge,
And gather by him, as he is behaved,
If 't be the affliction of his love or no,
That thus he suffers for.

QUEEN: I shall obey you.
And for your part, Ophelia, I do wish
That your good beauties be the happy cause
Of Hamlet's wildness: so shall I hope your virtues
Will bring him to his wonted way again,
To both your honours.

OPHELIA: Madam, I wish it may.

Exit Queen Gertrude

POLONIUS: Ophelia, walk you here. Gracious, so please you,
We will bestow ourselves. Read on this book;
That show of such an exercise may colour,
Your loneliness. We are oft to blame in this,
'Tis too much proved—that with devotion's visage

And pious action we do sugar o'er
The devil himself.

KING: O, 'tis too true!
How smart a lash that speech doth give my conscience!
The harlot's cheek, beautied with plastering art,
Is not more ugly to the thing that helps it
Than is my deed to my most painted word:
O heavy burthen!

POLONIUS: I hear him coming: let's withdraw, my Lord.

Exeunt King Claudius and Polonius

Enter Hamlet

HAMET: To be, or not to be: that is the question:
Whether 'tis nobler in the mind to suffer
The slings and arrows of outrageous fortune,
Or to take arms against a sea of troubles,
And by opposing end them? To die: to sleep;
No more; and by a sleep to say we end
The heart-ache and the thousand natural shocks
That flesh is heir to, 'tis a consummation
Devoutly to be wish'd. To die, to sleep;
To sleep: perchance to dream: ay, there's the rub;
For in that sleep of death what dreams may come,
When we have shuffled off this mortal coil,
Must give us pause: there's the respect
That makes calamity of so long life;
For who would bear the whips and scorns of time,

The oppressor's wrong, the proud man's contumely,
The pangs of despised love, the law's delay,
The insolence of office and the spurns
That patient merit of the unworthy takes,
When he himself might his quietus make,
With a bare bodkin? who would fardels bear,
To grunt and sweat under a weary life,
But that the dread of something after death,
The undiscover'd country from whose bourn
No traveller returns, puzzles the will,
And makes us rather bear those ills we have
Than fly to others that we know not of?
Thus conscience does make cowards of us all;
And thus the native hue of resolution
Is sicklied o'er with the pale cast of thought,
And enterprises of great pith and moment,
With this regard their currents turn awry,
And lose the name of action. Soft you now!
The fair Ophelia! Nymph, in thy orisons
Be all my sins remember'd.

OPHELIA: Good my Lord,
How does your honour for this many a day?

HAMLET: I humbly thank you; well, well, well.

OPHELIA: My Lord, I have remembrances of yours,
That I have longed long to re-deliver;
I pray you, now receive them.

HAMLET: No, not I;
I never gave you aught.

OPHELIA: My honour'd Lord, you know right well you did;
And, with them, words of so sweet breath composed
As made the things more rich: their perfume lost,
Take these again; for to the noble mind,
Rich gifts wax poor when givers prove unkind.
There, my Lord.

HAMLET: Ha, ha! are you honest?

OPHELIA: My Lord?

HAMLET: Are you fair?

OPHELIA: What means your Lordship?

HAMLET: That if you be honest and fair, your honesty should admit no discourse to your beauty.

OPHELIA: Could beauty, my Lord, have better commerce than with honesty?

HAMLET: Ay, truly; for the power of beauty will sooner transform honesty from what it is to a bawd than the force of honesty can translate beauty into his likeness: this was some time a paradox, but now the time gives it proof. I did love you once.

OPHELIA: Indeed, my Lord, you made me believe so.

HAMLET: You should not have believed me; for virtue cannot so inoculate our old stock but we shall relish of it: I loved you not.

OPHELIA: I was the more deceived.

HAMLET: Get thee to a nunnery: why wouldst thou be a

breeder of sinners? I am myself indifferent honest; but yet I could accuse me of such things that it were better my mother had not borne me: I am very proud, revengeful, ambitious, with more offences at my beck than I have thoughts to put them in, imagination to give them shape, or time to act them in. What should such fellows as I do crawling between earth and heaven? We are arrant knaves, all; believe none of us. Go thy ways to a nunnery. Where's your father?

OPHELIA: At home, my Lord.

HAMLET: Let the doors be shut upon him, that he may play the fool no where but in's own house. Farewell.

OPHELIA: O, help him, you sweet heavens!

HAMLET: If thou dost marry, I'll give thee this plague for thy dowry: be thou as chaste as ice, as pure as snow, thou shalt not escape calumny. Get thee to a nunnery, go: farewell. Or, if thou wilt needs marry, marry a fool; for wise men know well enough what monsters you make of them. To a nunnery, go, and quickly too. Farewell.

OPHELIA: O heavenly powers, restore him!

HAMLET: I have heard of your paintings too, well enough; God has given you one face, and you make yourselves another: you jig, you amble, and you lisp, and nick-name God's creatures, and make your wantonness your ignorance. Go to, I'll no more on't; it hath made me mad. I say, we will have no more marriages: those that are married already, all but one, shall live; the rest shall keep as they are. To a nunnery, go.

Exit Hamlet

OPHELIA: O, what a noble mind is here o'erthrown!
The courtier's, soldier's, scholar's eye, tongue, sword;
Th' expectancy and rose of the fair state,
The glass of fashion and the mould of form,
Th' observ'd of all observers, quite, quite down!
And I, of ladies most deject and wretched,
That suck'd the honey of his music vows,
Now see that noble and most sovereign reason,
Like sweet bells jangled, out of tune and harsh;
That unmatch'd form and feature of blown youth
Blasted with ecstasy: O, woe is me,
To have seen what I have seen, see what I see!

Enter King Claudius and Polonius

KING: Love! his affections do not that way tend;
Nor what he spake, though it lack'd form a little,
Was not like madness. There's something in his soul,
O'er which his melancholy sits on brood;
And I do doubt the hatch and the disclose
Will be some danger: which for to prevent,
I have in quick determination
Thus set it down: he shall with speed to England,
For the demand of our neglected tribute:
Haply the seas and countries different
With variable objects shall expel
This something-settled matter in his heart,

Whereon his brains still beating puts him thus
From fashion of himself. What think you on't?

POLONIUS: It shall do well: but yet do I believe
The origin and commencement of his grief
Sprung from neglected love. How now, Ophelia!
You need not tell us what Lord Hamlet said;
We heard it all. My Lord, do as you please;
But, if you hold it fit, after the play
Let his Queen mother all alone entreat him
To show his grief: let her be round with him;
And I'll be placed, so please you, in the ear
Of all their conference. If she find him not,
To England send him, or confine him where
Your wisdom best shall think.

KING: It shall be so:
Madness in great ones must not unwatch'd go.

Exeunt

III. 2

Enter Hamlet and Players

HAMLET: Speak the speech, I pray you, as I pronounced it to you, trippingly on the tongue: but if you mouth it, as many of your players do, I had as lief the town-crier spoke my lines. Nor do not saw the air too much with your hand, thus, but use all gently; for in the very torrent, tempest, and, as I may say, the whirlwind of passion, you must acquire and beget a temperance that may give it smoothness. O, it offends me to the soul to hear a robustious periwig-pated fellow tear a passion to tatters, to very rags, to split the ears of the groundlings, who for the most part , are capable of nothing but inexplicable dumbshows and noise: I would have such a fellow whipped for o'erdoing Termagant; it out-herods Herod: pray you, avoid it.

PLAYER: I warrant your honour.

HAMLET: Be not too tame neither, but let your own discretion be your tutor: suit the action to the word, the word to the action; with this special observance that you o'erstep not the modesty of nature: for any thing so overdone is from the purpose of playing, whose end, both at the first and now, was and is, to hold, as 'twere, the mirror up to nature; to show virtue her own feature, scorn her own image, and the very age and body of the time his form and pressure. Now this overdone, or come tardy off, though it make the unskilful laugh, cannot but make the judicious grieve; the censure of the which one must in your allowance o'erweigh a whole theatre of others. O, there be players that I have seen play, and heard others praise, and that highly, not to speak it profanely, that, neither having the accent of Christians nor the gait of Christian, pagan, nor man, have so strutted and bellowed that I have thought some of nature's journeymen had made men and not made them well, they imitated humanity so abominably.

PLAYER: I hope we have reformed that indifferently with us, sir.

HAMLET: O, reform it altogether. And let those that play your clowns speak no more than is set down for them; for there be of them that will themselves laugh, to set on some quantity of barren spectators to laugh too; though, in the meantime, some necessary question of the play be then to be considered: that's villanous, and shows a most pitiful ambition in the fool that uses it. Go, make you ready.

Exeunt Players

Enter Polonius, Rosencrantz and Guildenstern

How now, my Lord! I will the King hear this piece of work?

POLONIUS: And the Queen too, and that presently.

HAMLET: Bid the players make haste.

Exit Polonius

Will you two help to hasten them?

BOTH: We will, my Lord.

Exeunt Rosencrantz and Guildenstern

Enter Horatio

HAMLET: What ho! Horatio!

HORATIO: Here, sweet Lord, at your service.

HAMLET: Horatio, thou art e'en as just a man
As e'er my conversation cop'd withal.

HORATIO: O, my dear Lord,

HAMLET: Nay, do not think I flatter;
For what advancement may I hope from thee
That no revenue hast but thy good spirits,
To feed and clothe thee? Why should the poor be flatter'd?
No, let the candied tongue lick absurd pomp,
And crook the pregnant hinges of the knee,
Where thrift may follow fawning. Dost thou hear?
Since my dear soul was mistress of her choice
And could of men distinguish, her election
Hath seal'd thee for herself; for thou hast been
As one, in suffering all, that suffers nothing,
A man that fortune's buffets and rewards
Hast ta'en with equal thanks: and blest are those
Whose blood and judgment are so well commingled,
That they are not a pipe for fortune's finger
To sound what stop she please. Give me that man,
That is not passion's slave, and I will wear him
In my heart's core, ay, in my heart of heart,
As I do thee. Something too much of this.
There is a play to-night before the King;
One scene of it comes near the circumstance
Which I have told thee of my father's death:
I prithee, when thou seest that act afoot,
Even with the very comment of thy soul

Observe mine uncle: if his occulted guilt
Do not itself unkennel in one speech,
It is a damned ghost that we have seen,
And my imaginations are as foul
As Vulcan's stithy. Give him heedful note;
For I mine eyes will rivet to his face,
And after we will both our judgments join
In censure of his seeming.

HORATIO: Well, my Lord:
If he steal aught the whilst this play is playing,
And 'scape detecting, I will pay the theft.

HAMLET: They are coming to the play; I must be idle:
Get you a place.

Enter King, Queen, Polonius, Ophelia, Rosencrantz, Guildenstern, and others.

KING: How fares our cousin Hamlet?

HAMLET: Excellent, i' faith; of the chameleon's dish: I eat the air, promise-crammed: you cannot feed Capons so.

KING: I have nothing with this answer, Hamlet; these words are not mine.

HAMLET: No, nor mine now.
My Lord, you played once i' th' university, you say?

POLONIUS: That did I, my Lord; and was accounted a good actor.

HAMLET: What did you enact?

POLONIUS: I did enact Julius Caesar: I was killed i' th'

Capitol; Brutus killed me.

HAMLET: It was a brute part of him to kill so capital a calf there. Be the players ready?

ROSENCRANTZ: Ay, my Lord; they stay upon your patience.

QUEEN: Come hither, my dear Hamlet, sit by me.

HAMLET: No, good mother, here's metal more attractive.

POLONIUS: O, ho! do you mark that?

HAMLET: Lady, shall I lie in your lap?

OPHELIA: No, my Lord.

HAMLET: I mean, my head upon your lap?

OPHELIA: Ay, my Lord.

HAMLET: Do you think I meant country matters?

OPHELIA: I think nothing, my Lord.

HAMLET: That's a fair thought to lie between maids' legs.

OPHELIA: What is, my Lord?

HAMLET: Nothing.

OPHELIA: You are merry, my Lord.

HAMLET: Who, I?

OPHELIA: Ay, my Lord.

HAMLET: O God, your only jig-maker. What should a man do but be merry? for, look you, how cheerfully my mother looks, and my father died within these two hours.

OPHELIA: Nay, 'tis twice two months, my Lord.

HAMLET: So long? Nay then, let the devil wear black,

for I'll have a suit of sables. O heavens! die two months ago, and not forgotten yet? Then there's hope, a great man's memory may outlive his life half a year: but, by'r lady, he must build churches, then; or else shall he suffer not thinking on, with the hobby-horse, whose epitaph is 'For O, for O, the hobby-horse is forgot.'

Hautboys play. The dumb-show enters

Enter a King and a Queen very lovingly; the Queen embracing him, and he her. She kneels, and makes show of protestation unto him. He takes her up, and reclines his head upon her neck: lays him down upon a bank of flowers: she, seeing him asleep, leaves him. Anon comes in a fellow, takes off his crown, kisses it, and pours poison in the King's ears, and exit. The Queen returns; finds the King dead, and makes passionate action. The Poisoner, with some two or three Mutes, comes in again, seeming to lament with her. The dead body is carried away. The Poisoner wooes the Queen with gifts: she seems loath and unwilling awhile, but in the end accepts his love

Exeunt

OPHELIA: What means this, my Lord?

HAMLET: Marry, this is miching mallecho; it means mischief.

OPHELIA: Belike this show imports the argument of the play.

HAMLET: We shall know by this fellow: the players cannot keep counsel; they'll tell all.

OPHELIA: Will he tell us what this show meant?

HAMLET: Ay, or any show that you'll show him: be not you ashamed to show, he'll not shame to tell you what it means.

OPHELIA: You are naught, you are naught: I'll mark the play.

Enter Prologue

PROLOGUE: For us, and for our tragedy,
Here stooping to your clemency,
We beg your hearing patiently.

Exit

HAMLET: Is this a prologue, or the posy of a ring?

OPHELIA: 'Tis brief, my Lord.

HAMLET: As woman's love.

Enter two Players, King and Queen

PLAYER KING: Full thirty times hath Phoebus' cart gone round
Neptune's salt wash and Tellus' orbed ground,
And thirty dozen moons with borrow'd sheen,
About the world have times twelve thirties been,
Since love our hearts and Hymen did our hands
Unite commutual in most sacred bands.

PLAYER QUEEN: So many journeys may the sun and moon
Make us again count o'er ere love be done!
But, woe is me, you are so sick of late,
So far from cheer and from your former state,
That I distrust you. Yet, though I distrust,
Discomfort you, my Lord, it nothing must:

For women's fear and love holds quantity;
In neither aught, or in extremity.
Now, what my love is, proof hath made you know;
And as my love is sized, my fear is so:
Where love is great, the littlest doubts are fear;
Where little fears grow great, great love grows there.

PLAYER KING: 'Faith, I must leave thee, love, and shortly too;
My operant powers their functions leave to do:
And thou shalt live in this fair world behind,
Honour'd, beloved; and haply one as kind
For husband shalt thou.

PLAYER QUEEN: O, confound the rest!
Such love, must needs be treason in my breast:
In second husband let me be accurst!
None wed the second but who kill'd the first.

HAMLET: (Aside) Wormwood, wormwood.

PLAYER QUEEN: The instances that second marriage move
Are base respects of thrift, but none of love:
A second time, I kill my husband dead,
When second husband kisses me in bed.

PLAYER KING: I do believe you think what now you speak;
But what we do determine oft we break.
Purpose is but the slave to memory,
Of violent birth, but poor validity;
Which now, like fruit unripe, sticks on the tree;
But fall, unshaken, when they mellow be.

Most necessary 'tis that we forget
To pay ourselves what to ourselves is debt:
What to ourselves in passion we propose,
The passion ending, doth the purpose lose.
The violence of either grief or joy
Their own enactures with themselves destroy:
Where joy most revels, grief doth most lament;
Grief joys, joy grieves, on slender accident.
This world is not for aye, nor 'tis not strange
That even our loves should with our fortunes change;
For 'tis a question left us yet to prove,
Whether love lead fortune, or else fortune love.
The great man down, you mark his favourite flies;
The poor advanced makes friends of enemies.
And hitherto doth love on fortune tend;
For who not needs shall never lack a friend,
And who in want a hollow friend doth try,
Directly seasons him his enemy.
But, orderly to end where I begun,
Our wills and fates do so contrary run
That our devices still are overthrown;
Our thoughts are ours, their ends none of our own:
So think thou wilt no second husband wed;
But die thy thoughts when thy first lord is dead.

PLAYER QUEEN: Nor earth to me give food, nor heaven light!
Sport and repose lock from me day and night!

To desperation turn my trust and hope!
An anchor's cheer in prison be my scope!
Each opposite that blanks the face of joy,
Meet what I would have well and it destroy!
Both here and hence pursue me lasting strife,
If, once a widow, ever I be wife!

HAMLET: If she should break it now!

PLAYER KING: 'Tis deeply sworn. Sweet, leave me here awhile;
My spirits grow dull, and fain I would beguile
The tedious day with sleep.

Sleeps

PLAYER QUEEN: Sleep rock thy brain,
And never come mischance between us twain!

Exit

HAMLET: Madam, how like you this play?

QUEEN: The lady protests too much, methinks.

HAMLET: O, but she'll keep her word.

KING: Have you heard the argument? Is there no offence in 't?

HAMLET: No, no, they do but jest, poison in jest; no offence i' th' world.

KING: What do you call the play?

HAMLET: The Mouse-trap. Marry, how? Tropically. This play is the image of a murder done in Vienna: Gonzago is the Duke's name; his wife, Baptista: you shall see anon; 'tis a knavish piece of work: but what o' that? Your majesty and we that have free souls, it touches us not: let the galled jade wince, our withers are unwrung.

Enter Lucianus

This is one Lucianus, nephew to the King.

OPHELIA: You are as good as a chorus, my Lord.

HAMLET: I could interpret between you and your love, if I could see the puppets dallying.

OPHELIA: You are keen, my Lord, you are keen.

HAMLET: It would cost you a groaning to take off my edge.

OPHELIA: Still better, and worse.

HAMLET: So you must take your husbands. Begin murderer; pox, leave thy damnable faces, and begin. Come: 'the croaking raven doth bellow for revenge.'

LUCIANUS: Thoughts black, hands apt, drugs fit, and
time agreeing;
Confederate season, else no creature seeing;
Thou mixture rank, of midnight weeds collected,
With Hecate's ban thrice blasted, thrice infected,
Thy natural magic and dire property,
On wholesome life usurp immediately.

Pours the poison into the sleeper's ears

HAMLET: He poisons him i' th' garden for's estate. His name's Gonzago: the story is extant, and writ in choice Italian: you shall see anon how the murderer gets the love of Gonzago's wife.

OPHELIA: The King rises.

HAMLET: What, frighted with false fire!

QUEEN: How fares my Lord?

POLONIUS: Give o'er the play.

KING: Give me some light: away!

ALL: Lights, lights, lights!

Exeunt all but Hamlet and Horatio

HAMLET: Why, let the stricken deer go weep,
The hart ungalled play;
For some must watch, while some must sleep:
So runs the world away.
Would not this, sir, and a forest of feathers— if the rest of my fortunes turn Turk with me—with two Provincial roses on my razed shoes, get me a fellowship in a cry of players, sir?

HORATIO: Half a share.

HAMLET: A whole one, I.
For thou dost know, O Damon dear,
This realm dismantled was
Of Jove himself; and now reigns here
A very, very—pajock.

HORATIO: You might have rhymed.

HAMLET: O good Horatio, I'll take the ghost's word for a thousand pound. Didst perceive?

HORATIO: Very well, my Lord.

HAMLET: Upon the talk of the poisoning?

HORATIO: I did very well note him.

HAMLET: Ah, ha! Come, some music! Come, the recorders!
For if the King like not the comedy,
Why then, belike, he likes it not, perdy.
Come, some music!

Enter Rosencrantz and Guildenstern

GUILDENSTERN: Good my Lord, vouchsafe me a word with you.

HAMLET: Sir, a whole history.

GUILDENSTERN: The King, sir,

HAMLET: Ay, sir, what of him?

GUILDENSTERN: Is in his retirement, marvellous distempered.

HAMLET: With drink, sir?

GUILDENSTERN: No, my Lord, rather with choler.

HAMLET: Your wisdom should show itself more richer to signify this to his doctor; for, for me to put him to his purgation would perhaps plunge him into far more choler.

GUILDENSTERN: Good my Lord, put your discourse into some frame and start not so wildly from my affair.

HAMLET: I am tame, sir: pronounce.

GUILDENSTERN: The Queen, your mother, in most great affliction of spirit, hath sent me to you.

HAMLET: You are welcome.

GUILDENSTERN: Nay, good my Lord, this courtesy is not of the right breed. If it shall please you to make me a wholesome answer, I will do your mother's commandment: if not, your pardon and my return shall be the end of my business.

HAMLET: Sir, I cannot.

GUILDENSTERN: What, my Lord?

HAMLET: Make you a wholesome answer; my wit's diseased: but, sir, such answer as I can make, you shall command; or, rather, as you say, my mother: therefore no more, but to the matter: my mother, you say.

ROSENCRANTZ: Then thus she says; your behaviour hath struck her into amazement and admiration.

HAMLET: O wonderful son, that can so astonish a mother! But is there no sequel at the heels of this mother's admiration?

ROSENCRANTZ: She desires to speak with you in her closet, ere you go to bed.

HAMLET: We shall obey, were she ten times our mother. Have you any further trade with us?

ROSENCRANTZ: My Lord, you once did love me.

HAMLET: So I do still, by these pickers and stealers.

ROSENCRANTZ: Good my Lord, what is your cause of distemper? You do, surely, bar the door upon your own liberty, if you deny your griefs to your friend.

HAMLET: Sir, I lack advancement.

ROSENCRANTZ: How can that be, when you have the voice of the king himself for your succession in Denmark?

HAMLET: Ay, but sir, 'While the grass grows,'—the proverb is something musty.

Enter Players with recorders

O, the recorders! let me see one. To withdraw with you: why do you go about to recover the wind of me, as if you would drive me into a toil?

GUILDENSTERN: O, my Lord, if my duty be too bold, my love is too unmannerly.

HAMLET: I do not well understand that. Will you play upon this pipe?

GUILDENSTERN: My Lord, I cannot.

HAMLET: I pray you.

GUILDENSTERN: Believe me, I cannot.

HAMLET: I do beseech you.

GUILDENSTERN: I know no touch of it, my Lord.

HAMLET: 'Tis as easy as lying: govern these ventages with your fingers and thumb, give it breath with your mouth, and it will discourse most eloquent music. Look you, these are the stops.

GUILDENSTERN: But these cannot I command to any utterance of harmony; I have not the skill.

HAMLET: Why, look you now, how unworthy a thing you make of me! You would play upon me; you would seem to know my stops; you would pluck out the heart of my mystery; you would sound me from my lowest note to the top of my compass: and there is much music, excellent voice, in this little organ; yet cannot you make it speak. Why, do you think I am easier to be played on than a pipe? Call me what instrument you will, though you can fret me, yet you cannot play upon me.

God bless you, sir!

Enter Polonius

POLONIUS: My Lord, the Queen would speak with you, and presently.

HAMLET: Do you see yonder cloud that's almost in shape of a camel?

POLONIUS: By the mass, and 'tis like a camel, indeed.

HAMLET: Methinks it is like a weazel.

POLONIUS: It is backed like a weazel.

HAMLET: Or like a whale?

POLONIUS: Very like a whale.

HAMLET: Then I will come to my mother by and by. They fool me to the top of my bent. I will come by and by.

POLONIUS: I will say so.

HAMLET: By and by is easily said.

Exit Polonius

Leave me, friends.

Exeunt all but Hamlet

'Tis now the very witching time of night,
When churchyards yawn and hell itself breathes out
Contagion to this world: now could I drink hot blood,
And do such bitter business as the day
Would quake to look on. Soft! now to my mother.
O heart, lose not thy nature; let not ever
The soul of Nero enter this firm bosom:
Let me be cruel, not unnatural:

I will speak daggers to her, but use none;
My tongue and soul in this be hypocrites;
How in my words soever she be shent,
To give them seals never, my soul, consent!

Exeunt

III. 3

Enter King Claudius, Rosencrantz, and Guildenstern

KING: I like him not, nor stands it safe with us
To let his madness range. Therefore prepare you;
I your commission will forthwith dispatch,
And he to England shall along with you:
The terms of our estate may not endure
Hazard so dangerous as doth hourly grow
Out of his lunacies.

GUILDENSTERN: We will ourselves provide:
Most holy and religious fear it is
To keep those many many bodies safe
That live and feed upon your Majesty.

ROSENCRANTZ: The single and peculiar life is bound,
With all the strength and armour of the mind,
To keep itself from noyance; but much more,
That spirit upon whose weal depends and rest
The lives of many. The cease of Majesty
Dies not alone; but, like a gulf, doth draw
What's near it with it: it is a massy wheel,

Fix'd on the summit of the highest mount,
To whose huge spokes ten thousand lesser things
Are mortis'd and adjoin'd; which, when it falls,
Each small annexment, petty consequence,
Attends the boisterous ruin. Never alone
Did the King sigh, but with a general groan.

KING: Arm you, I pray you, to this speedy voyage;
For we will fetters put upon this fear,
Which now goes too free-footed.

BOTH: We will haste us.

Exeunt

Enter Polonius

POLONIUS: My Lord, he's going to his mother's closet:
Behind the arras I'll convey myself,
To hear the process; and warrant she'll tax him home:
And, as you said, and wisely was it said,
'Tis meet that some more audience than a mother,
Since nature makes them partial, should o'erhear
The speech, of vantage. Fare you well, my liege:
I'll call upon you ere you go to bed,
And tell you what I know.

KING: Thanks, dear my Lord.

Exit Polonius

O, my offence is rank it smells to heaven;
It hath the primal eldest curse upon't,
A brother's murder. Pray can I not,

Though inclination be as sharp as will:
My stronger guilt defeats my strong intent;
And, like a man to double business bound,
I stand in pause where I shall first begin,
And both neglect. What if this cursed hand
Were thicker than itself with brother's blood,
Is there not rain enough in the sweet heavens
To wash it white as snow? Whereto serves mercy
But to confront the visage of offence?
And what's in prayer but this two-fold force,
To be forestalled ere we come to fall,
Or pardon'd being down? Then I'll look up;
My fault is past. But, O, what form of prayer
Can serve my turn? 'Forgive me my foul murder'?
That cannot be; since I am still possess'd
Of those effects for which I did the murder,
My crown, mine own ambition and my Queen.
May one be pardon'd and retain the offence?
In the corrupted currents of this world
Offence's gilded hand may shove by justice,
And oft 'tis seen the wicked prize itself
Buys out the law: but 'tis not so above;
There is no shuffling, there the action lies
In his true nature; and we ourselves compell'd,
Even to the teeth and forehead of our faults,
To give in evidence. What then? what rests?

Try what repentance can: what can it not?
Yet what can it when one cannot repent?
O wretched state! O bosom black as death!
O limed soul, that, struggling to be free,
Art more engaged! Help, angels! Make assay!
Bow, stubborn knees; and, heart with strings of steel,
Be soft as sinews of the newborn babe!
All may be well.

The King retires and kneels. Enter Hamlet

HAMLET: Now might I do it pat, now he is praying;
And now I'll do't. And so he goes to heaven;
And so am I revenged. That would be scann'd:
A villain kills my father; and for that,
I, his sole son, do this same villain send
To heaven.
O, this is hire and salary, not revenge.
He took my father grossly, full of bread;
With all his crimes broad blown, as flush as May;
And how his audit stands who knows save heaven?
But in our circumstance and course of thought,
'Tis heavy with him: and am I then revenged,
To take him in the purging of his soul,
When he is fit and season'd for his passage?
No!
Up, sword; and know thou a more horrid hent:
When he is drunk asleep, or in his rage,

Or in the incestuous pleasure of his bed;
At gaming, swearing, or about some act
That has no relish of salvation in't;
Then trip him, that his heels may kick at heaven,
And that his soul may be as damn'd and black
As hell, whereto it goes. My mother stays:
This physic but prolongs thy sickly days.

KING: My words fly up, my thoughts remain below:
Words without thoughts never to heaven go.

Exeunt

III. 4

Enter Queen and Polonius

POLONIUS: He will come straight. Look you lay home to him:
Tell him his pranks have been too broad to bear with,
And that your grace hath screen'd and stood between
Much heat and him. I'll silence me even here.
Pray you, be round with him.

HAMLET: Mother, mother, mother!

QUEEN: I'll warrant you,
Fear me not: withdraw, I hear him coming.

Enter Hamlet

HAMLET: Now, mother, what's the matter?

QUEEN: Hamlet, thou hast thy father much offended.

HAMLET: Mother, you have my father much offended.

QUEEN: Come, come, you answer with an idle tongue.
HAMLET: Go, go, you question with an idle tongue.
QUEEN: Why, how now, Hamlet!
HAMLET: What's the matter now?
QUEEN: Have you forgot me?
HAMLET: No, by the Rood, not so:
You are the Queen, your husband's brother's wife;
And—would it were not so!—you are my mother.
QUEEN: Nay, then, I'll set those to you that can speak.
HAMLET: Come, come, and sit you down; you shall not budge;
You go not till I set you up a glass,
Where you may see the inmost part of you.
QUEEN: What wilt thou do? Thou wilt not murder me?
Help, help, ho!
POLONIUS: (Behind) What, ho! help, help, help!
HAMLET: How now! a rat? Dead, for a ducat, dead!

Kills Polonius

POLONIUS: O, I am slain!

Falls and dies

QUEEN: O me, what hast thou done?
HAMLET: Nay, I know not: Is it the King?
QUEEN: O, what a rash and bloody deed is this!
HAMLET: A bloody deed! almost as bad, good mother,
As kill a king, and marry with his brother.
QUEEN: As kill a King!

HAMLET: Ay, lady, 'twas my word.
Thou wretched, rash, intruding fool, farewell!
I took thee for thy better: take thy fortune;
Thou find'st to be too busy, is some danger.
Leave wringing of your hands: peace! sit you down,
And let me wring your heart; for so I shall,
If it be made of penetrable stuff,
If damned custom have not braz'd it so,
That it is proof and bulwark against sense.

QUEEN: What have I done, that thou darest wag thy tongue
In noise so rude against me?

HAMLET: Such an act
That blurs the grace and blush of modesty,
Calls Virtue hypocrite, takes off the rose
From the fair forehead of an innocent love,
And sets a blister there, makes marriage-vows
As false as dicers' oaths: O, such a deed,
As from the body of contraction plucks
The very soul, and sweet religion makes
A rhapsody of words: heaven's face doth glow:
Yea, this solidity and compound mass,
With tristful visage, as against the doom,
Is thought-sick at the act.

QUEEN: Ay me, what act,
That roars so loud, and thunders in the index?

HAMLET: Look here, upon this picture, and on this,
The counterfeit presentment of two brothers.
See, what a grace was seated on this brow;
Hyperion's curls; the front of Jove himself;
An eye like Mars, to threaten and command;
A station like the herald Mercury,
New-lighted on a heaven-kissing hill;
A combination and a form indeed,
Where every god did seem to set his seal,
To give the world assurance of a man:
This was your husband. Look you now, what follows:
Here is your husband; like a mildew'd ear,
Blasting his wholesome brother. Have you eyes?
Could you on this fair mountain leave to feed,
And batten on this moor? Ha! have you eyes?
You cannot call it love; for at your age,
The hey-day in the blood is tame, it's humble,
And waits upon the judgment: and what judgment
Would step from this to this? Sense, sure, you have,
Else could you not have motion; but sure, that sense
Is apoplex'd; for madness would not err,
Nor sense to ecstasy was ne'er so thrall'd
But it reserved some quantity of choice,
To serve in such a difference. What devil was't
That thus hath cozen'd you at hoodman-blind?

Eyes without feeling, feeling without sight,
Ears without hands or eyes, smelling sans all,
Or but a sickly part of one true sense
Could not so mope.
O shame! where is thy blush? Rebellious hell,
If thou canst mutine in a matron's bones,
To flaming youth let virtue be as wax,
And melt in her own fire: proclaim no shame
When the compulsive ardour gives the charge,
Since frost itself as actively doth burn
And reason panders will.

QUEEN: O Hamlet, speak no more:
Thou turn'st mine eyes into my very soul;
And there I see such black and grained spots,
As will not leave their tinct.

HAMLET: Nay, but to live
In the rank sweat of an enseamed bed,
Stew'd in corruption, honeying and making love
Over the nasty sty.

QUEEN: O, speak to me no more;
These words, like daggers, enter in mine ears;
No more, sweet Hamlet!

HAMLET: A murderer and a villain;
A slave that is not twentieth part the tithe
Of your precedent lord; a vice of Kings;
A cutpurse of the empire and the rule,

That from a shelf the precious diadem stole,
And put it in his pocket!
QUEEN: No more!

Enter Ghost

HAMLET: A King of shreds and patches,—
Save me, and hover o'er me with your wings,
You heavenly guards! What would your gracious figure?
QUEEN: Alas, he's mad!
HAMLET: Do you not come your tardy son to chide,
That, lapsed in time and passion, lets go by
The important acting of your dread command? O, say!
GHOST: Do not forget: this visitation
Is but to whet thy almost blunted purpose.
But, look, amazement on thy mother sits:
O, step between her and her fighting soul:
Conceit in weakest bodies, strongest works:
Speak to her, Hamlet.
HAMLET: How is it with you, Lady?
QUEEN: Alas, how is't with you,
That you do bend your eye on vacancy
And with the incorporal air do hold discourse.
Forth at your eyes your spirits wildly peep;
And, as the sleeping soldiers in th' alarm,
Your bedded hair, like life in excrements,
Start up, and stand on end. O gentle son,
Upon the heat and flame of thy distemper

Sprinkle cool patience. Whereon do you look?

HAMLET: On him, on him! Look you, how pale he glares!
His form and cause conjoin'd, preaching to stones,
Would make them capable. Do not look upon me;
Lest with this piteous action you convert
My stern effects: then what I have to do,
Will want true colour; tears perchance for blood.

QUEEN: To whom do you speak this?

HAMLET: Do you see nothing there?

QUEEN: Nothing at all; yet all that is I see.

HAMLET: Nor did you nothing hear?

QUEEN: No, nothing but ourselves.

HAMLET: Why, look you there! look, how it steals away!
My father, in his habit as he lived!
Look, where he goes, even now, out at the portal!

Exit Ghost

QUEEN: This the very coinage of your brain:
This bodiless creation ecstasy
Is very cunning in.

HAMLET: Ecstasy!
My pulse, as yours, doth temperately keep time,
And makes as healthful music: it is not madness
That I have utter'd: bring me to the test,
And I the matter will re-word; which madness
Would gambol from. Mother, for love of Grace,

Lay not a flattering unction to your soul,
That not your trespass, but my madness speaks:
It will but skin and film the ulcerous place,
Whilst rank corruption, mining all within,
Infects unseen. Confess yourself to heaven;
Repent what's past; avoid what is to come;
And do not spread the compost on the weeds,
To make them ranker. Forgive me this my virtue;
For in the fatness of these pursy times,
Virtue itself of vice must pardon beg,
Yea, curb and woo for leave to do him good.

QUEEN: O Hamlet, thou hast cleft my heart in twain.

HAMLET: O, throw away the worser part of it,
And live the purer with the other half.
Good night: but go not to mine uncle's bed;
Assume a virtue, if you have it not.
That monster, custom, who all sense doth eat,
Of habits devil, is angel yet in this,
That to the use of actions fair and good
He likewise gives a frock or livery,
That aptly is put on. Refrain to-night,
And that shall lend a kind of easiness
To the next abstinence: the next more easy;
For use almost can change the stamp of nature,
And either the devil, or throw him out
With wondrous potency. Once more, good night:

And when you are desirous to be bless'd,
I'll blessing beg of you. For this same lord,
I do repent: but heaven hath pleased it so,
To punish me with this and this with me,
That I must be their scourge and minister.
I will bestow him, and will answer well
The death I gave him. So, again, good night.
I must be cruel, only to be kind:
Thus bad begins and worse remains behind.
One word more, good lady.

QUEEN: What shall I do?

HAMLET: Not this, by no means, that I bid you do:
Let the bloat King tempt you again to bed;
Pinch wanton on your cheek; call you his mouse;
And let him, for a pair of reechy kisses,
Or paddling in your neck with his damn'd fingers,
Make you to ravel all this matter out,
That I essentially am not in madness,
But mad in craft. 'Twere good you let him know;
For who, that's but a Queen, fair, sober, wise,
Would from a paddock, from a bat, a gib,
Such dear concernings hide? who would do so?
No, in despite of sense and secrecy,
Unpeg the basket on the house's top.
Let the birds fly, and, like the famous ape,
To try conclusions, in the basket creep,

And break your own neck down.
QUEEN: Be thou assured, if words be made of breath,
And breath of life, I have no life to breathe
What thou hast said to me.
HAMLET: I must to England; you know that?
QUEEN: Alack,
I had forgot: 'tis so concluded on.
HAMLET: There's letters seal'd: and my two schoolfellows,
Whom I will trust as I will adders fang'd,
They bear the mandate; they must sweep my way,
And marshal me to knavery. Let it work;
For 'tis the sport to have the engineer
Hoist with his own petard: and 't shall go hard
But I will delve one yard below their mines,
And blow them at the moon: O, 'tis most sweet,
When in one line two crafts directly meet.
This man shall set me packing:
I'll lug the guts into the neighbour room.
Mother, good night. Indeed this counsellor
Is now most still, most secret and most grave,
Who was in life a foolish prating knave.
Come, sir, to draw toward an end with you.
Good night, mother.

Exeunt Hamlet dragging in Polonius

IV. 1

Enter King

KING: There's matter in these sighs, these profound heaves:
You must translate: 'tis fit we understand them.
Where is your son?
QUEEN: Ah, my good Lord, what have I seen to-night!
KING: What, Gertrude? How does Hamlet?
QUEEN: Mad as the sea and wind, when both contend
Which is the mightier: in his lawless fit,
Behind the arras hearing something stir,
He whips out his rapier, and cries, 'A rat, a rat!'
And, in this brainish apprehension, kills
The unseen good old man.
KING: O heavy deed!
It had been so with us, had we been there:
His liberty is full of threats to all;
To you yourself, to us, to every one.
Alas, how shall this bloody deed be answer'd?
It will be laid to us, whose providence
Should have kept short, restrain'd and out of haunt,
This mad young man: but so much was our love,
We would not understand what was most fit;
But, like the owner of a foul disease,
To keep it from divulging, lets it feed
Even on the pith of life. Where is he gone?

QUEEN: To draw apart the body he hath kill'd:
O'er whom his very madness, like some ore
Among a mineral of metals base,
Shows itself pure; he weeps for what is done.
KING: O Gertrude, come away!
The sun no sooner shall the mountains touch,
But we will ship him hence: and this vile deed
We must, with all our majesty and skill,
Both countenance and excuse. Ho, Guildenstern!

Enter Rosencrantz and Guildenstern

Friends both, go join you with some further aid:
Hamlet in madness hath Polonius slain,
And from his mother's closet hath he dragg'd him:
Go seek him out; speak fair, and bring the body
Into the chapel. I pray you, haste in this.

Exeunt Rosencrantz and Guildenstern

Come, Gertrude, we'll call up our wisest friends;
And let them know, both what we mean to do,
And what's untimely done. O, come away!
My soul is full of discord and dismay.

Exeunt

IV. 2

Enter Hamlet

HAMLET: Safely stowed.
ROSENCRANTZ: }
GUILDENSTERN: } *[Within]* Hamlet! Lord Hamlet!

HAMLET: What noise? Who calls on Hamlet?
O, here they come.

Enter Rosencrantz and Guildenstern

ROSENCRANTZ: What have you done, my Lord, with the dead body?

HAMLET: Compounded it with dust, whereto 'tis kin.

ROSENCRANTZ: Tell us where 'tis, that we may take it thence
And bear it to the chapel.

HAMLET: Do not believe it.

ROSENCRANTZ: Believe what?

HAMLET: That I can keep your counsel and not mine own. Besides, to be demanded of a sponge! what replication should be made by the son of a King?

ROSENCRANTZ: Take you me for a sponge, my Lord?

HAMLET: Ay, sir, that soaks up the King's countenance, his rewards, his authorities. But such officers do the King best service in the end: he keeps them, like an ape, in the corner of his jaw; first mouthed, to be last swallowed: when he needs what you have glean'd, it is but squeezing you, and, sponge, you shall be dry again.

ROSENCRANTZ: I understand you not, my Lord.

HAMLET: I am glad of it: a knavish speech sleeps in a foolish ear.

ROSENCRANTZ: My Lord, you must tell us where the body is, and go with us to the King.

HAMLET: The body is with the King, but the King is not with the body. The King is a thing

GUILDENSTERN: A thing, my Lord!

HAMLET: Of nothing: bring me to him. Hide fox, and all after.

Exeunt

IV. 3

Enter King Claudius.

KING: I have sent to seek him, and to find the body.
How dangerous is it that this man goes loose!
Yet must not we put the strong law on him:
He's loved of the distracted multitude,
Who like not in their judgment, but their eyes;
And where, tis so, th' offender's scourge is weigh'd,
But never the offence. To bear all smooth and even,
This sudden sending him away must seem
Deliberate pause: diseases desperate grown
By desperate appliance are relieved,
Or not at all.

Enter Rosencrantz

How now! what hath befall'n?

ROSENCRANTZ: Where the dead body is bestow'd, my Lord,
We cannot get from him.

KING: But where is he?

ROSENCRANTZ: Without, my Lord; guarded, to know

your pleasure.

KING: Bring him before us.

ROSENCRANTZ: Ho, Guildenstern! bring in my Lord.

Enter Hamlet and Guildenstern

KING: Now, Hamlet, where's Polonius?

HAMLET: At supper.

KING: At supper! where?

HAMLET: Not where he eats, but where he is eaten: a certain convocation of politic worms are e'en at him. Your worm is your only emperor for diet: we fat all creatures else to fat us, and we fat ourselves for maggots: your fat King and your lean beggar is but variable service, two dishes, but to one table: that's the end.

KING: Alas, alas!

HAMLET: A man may fish with the worm that hath eat of a King, and cat of the fish that hath fed of that worm.

KING: What dost you mean by this?

HAMLET: Nothing but to show you how a King may go a progress through the guts of a beggar.

KING: Where is Polonius?

HAMLET: In heaven; send hither to see: if your messenger find him not there, seek him i' th' other place yourself. But indeed, if you find him not within this month, you shall nose him as you go up the stairs into the lobby.

KING: Go seek him there.

HAMLET: He will stay till ye come.

KING: Hamlet, this deed, for thine especial safety,
Which we do tender, as we dearly grieve
For that which thou hast done, must send thee hence
With fiery quickness: therefore prepare thyself;
The bark is ready, and the wind at help,
Th' associates tend, and every thing is bent
For England.

HAMLET: For England!

KING: Ay, Hamlet.

HAMLET: Good.

KING: So is it, if thou knew'st our purposes.

HAMLET: I see a cherub that sees them. But, come; for England! Farewell, dear mother.

KING: Thy loving father, Hamlet.

HAMLET: My mother: father and mother is man and wife; man and wife is one flesh; and so, my mother. Come, for England!

Exit

KING: Follow him at foot; tempt him with speed aboard;
Delay it not; I'll have him hence to-night:
Away! for every thing is seal'd and done
That else leans on th' affair: pray you, make haste.
And, England, if my love thou hold'st at aught
As my great power thereof may give thee sense,

Since yet thy cicatrice looks raw and red
After the Danish sword, and thy free awe
Pays homage to us—thou mayst not coldly set
Our sovereign process; which imports at full,
By letters conjuring to that effect,
The present death of Hamlet. Do it, England;
For like the hectic in my blood he rages,
And thou must cure me: till I know 'tis done,
Howe'er my haps, my joys were ne'er begun.

Exeunt

IV. 4

Enter Fortinbras, with his army.

FORTINBRAS: Go, captain, from me greet the Danish king;
Tell him that, by his licence, Fortinbras
Craves the conveyance of a promised march
Over his kingdom. You know the rendezvous:
If that his majesty would aught with us,
We shall express our duty in his eye;
And let him know so.

CAPTAIN: I will do't, my Lord.

FORTINBRAS: Go softly on.

Exeunt Fortinbras and Soldiers

Enter Hamlet, Rosencrantz, Guildenstern, and others

HAMLET: Good sir, whose powers are these?

CAPTAIN: They are of Norway, sir.

HAMLET: How purpos'd, sir, I pray you?
CAPTAIN: Against some part of Poland.
HAMLET: Who commands them, sir?
CAPTAIN: The nephews to old Norway, Fortinbras.
HAMLET: Goes it against the main of Poland, sir,
Or for some frontier?
CAPTAIN: Truly to speak, and with no addition,
We go to gain a little patch of ground
That hath in it no profit but the name.
To pay five ducats, five, I would not farm it;
Nor will it yield to Norway or the Pole
A ranker rate, should it be sold in fee.
HAMLET: Why, then the Polack never will defend it.
CAPTAIN: Yes, it is already garrison'd.
HAMLET: Two thousand souls and twenty thousand ducats
Will not debate the question of this straw:
This is the imposthume of much wealth and peace,
That inward breaks, and shows no cause without
Why the man dies. I humbly thank you, sir.
CAPTAIN: God be wi' you, sir.

Exeunt

ROSENCRANTZ: Wilt please you go, my Lord?
HAMLET: I'll be with you straight, go a little before.

Exeunt all except Hamlet

How all occasions do inform against me,
And spur my dull revenge! What is a man,

If his chief good and market of his time
Be but to sleep and feed? A beast, no more.
Sure, he that made us with such large discourse,
Looking before and after, gave us not
That capability and god-like reason
To fust in us unus'd. Now, whether it be
Bestial oblivion, or some craven scruple
Of thinking too precisely on th' event,
A thought which, quarter'd, hath but one part wisdom
And ever three parts coward, I do not know
Why yet I live to say 'This thing's to do;'
Sith I have cause and will and strength and means
To do't. Examples gross as earth exhort me:
Witness this army of such mass and charge
Led by a delicate and tender prince,
Whose spirit with divine ambition puff'd
Makes mouths at the invisible event,
Exposing what is mortal and unsure
To all that fortune, death and danger dare,
Even for an egg-shell. Rightly to be great
Is not to stir without great argument,
But greatly to find quarrel in a straw
When honour's at the stake. How stand I then,
That have a father kill'd, a mother stain'd,
Excitements of my reason and my blood,
And let all sleep, while, to my shame, I see

The imminent death of twenty thousand men,
That, for a fantasy and trick of fame,
Go to their graves like beds, fight for a plot
Whereon the numbers cannot try the cause,
Which is not tomb enough and continent
To hide the slain? O, from this time forth,
My thoughts be bloody, or be nothing worth!

Exeunt

IV. 5

Enter Queen and Horatio.

QUEEN: I will not speak with her.

HORATIO: She is importunate, indeed distract:
Her mood will needs be pitied.

QUEEN: What would she have?

HORATIO: She speaks much of her father; says she hears
There's tricks i' th' world; and hems, and beats her heart;
Spurns enviously at straws; speaks things in doubt,
That carry but half sense: her speech is nothing,
Yet the unshaped use of it doth move
The hearers to collection; they aim at it,
And botch the words up fit to their own thoughts;
Which, as her winks, and nods, and gestures yield them,

Indeed would make one think there might be thought,
Though nothing sure, yet much unhappily.

QUEEN: 'Twere good she were spoken with; for she may strew
Dangerous conjectures in ill-breeding minds.
Let her come in.

Exit Horatio

To my sick soul, as sin's true nature is,
Each toy seems prologue to some great amiss:
So full of artless jealousy is guilt,
It spills itself in fearing to be spilt.

Re-enter Horatio, with Ophelia

OPHELIA: Where is the beauteous Majesty of Denmark?

QUEEN: How now, Ophelia!

OPHELIA: [Sings]

How should I your true love know
From another one?
By his cockle hat and staff,
And his sandal shoon.

QUEEN: Alas, sweet lady, what imports this song?

OPHELIA: Say you? nay, pray you, mark.

He is dead and gone, Lady,
He is dead and gone;
At his head a grass-green turf,
At his heels a stone.

QUEEN: Nay, but, Ophelia,

OPHELIA: Pray you, mark.

White his shroud as the mountain snow,

Enter King Claudius

QUEEN: Alas, look here, my Lord.

OPHELIA:

Larded with sweet flowers
Which bewept to the grave did go
With true-love showers.

KING: How do you, pretty Lady?

OPHELIA: Well, God 'ild you! They say the owl was a baker's daughter. Lord, we know what we are, but know not what we may be. God be at your table!

KING: Conceit upon her father.

OPHELIA: Pray you, let's have no words of this; but when they ask you what it means, say you this:

To-morrow is Saint Valentine's day,
All in the morning betime,
And I a maid at your window,
To be your Valentine.
Then up he rose, and donn'd his clothes,
And dupp'd the chamber-door;
Let in the maid, that out a maid
Never departed more.

KING: Pretty Ophelia!

OPHELIA: Indeed, la, without an oath, I'll make an end on't:

By Gis and by Saint Charity,
Alack, and fie for shame!
Young men will do't, if they come to't;
By cock, they are to blame.
Quoth she, before you tumbled me,
You promis'd me to wed.
So would I ha' done, by yonder sun,
And thou hadst not come to my bed.

KING: How long hath she been thus?

OPHELIA: I hope all will be well. We must be patient: but I cannot choose but weep, to think they should lay him i' th' cold ground. My brother shall know of it: and so I thank you for your good counsel. Come, my coach! Good night, ladies; good night, sweet ladies; good night, good night.

Exuant

KING: Follow her close; give her good watch,
I pray you.

Exit Horatio

O, this is the poison of deep grief; it springs
All from her father's death. O Gertrude, Gertrude,
When sorrows come, they come not single spies
But in battalions. First, her father slain:
Next, your son gone; and he most violent author
Of his own just remove: the people muddied,
Thick and unwholesome in their thoughts and whispers,

For good Polonius' death; and we have done but greenly,
In hugger-mugger to inter him: poor Ophelia
Divided from herself and her fair judgment,
Without the which we are pictures, or mere beasts:
Last, and as much containing as all these,
Her brother is in secret come from France;
Feeds on his wonder, keeps himself in clouds,
And wants not buzzers to infect his ear
With pestilent speeches of his father's death;
Wherein necessity, of matter beggar'd,
Will nothing stick our person to arraign
In ear and ear. O my dear Gertrude, this,
Like to a murdering-piece, in many places
Gives me superfluous death.

A noise within. Enter a Messenger.

QUEEN: Alack, what noise is this?
KING: Where are my Switzers? Let them guard the door.
What is the matter?
MESSENGER: Save yourself, my Lord:
The ocean, overpeering of his list,
Eats not the flats with more impetuous haste
Than young Laertes, in a riotous head,
O'erbears your officers. The rabble call him Lord;
And, as the world were now but to begin,
Antiquity forgot, custom not known,

The ratifiers and props of every word,
They cry 'Choose we: Laertes shall be King:'
Caps, hands, and tongues, applaud it to the clouds:
'Laertes shall be King, Laertes King!'

QUEEN: How cheerfully on the false trail they cry!
O, this is counter, you false Danish dogs!

Noise within

KING: The doors are broke.

Enter Laertes, armed; Danes following

LAERTES: Where is this King? Sirs, stand you all without.

ALL: No, let's come in.

LAERTES: I pray you, give me leave.

ALL: We will, we will.

Exeunt.

LAERTES: I thank you: keep the door. O thou vile King,
Give me my father!

QUEEN: Calmly, good Laertes.

LAERTES: That drop of blood that's calm proclaims me bastard,
Cries cuckold to my father, brands the harlot
Even here, between the chaste unsmirched brow
Of my true mother.

KING: What is the cause, Laertes,
That thy rebellion looks so giant-like?
Let him go, Gertrude; do not fear our person:
There's such divinity doth hedge a king,

That treason can but peep to what it would,
Acts little of his will. Tell me, Laertes,
Why thou art thus incensed. Let him go, Gertrude.
Speak, man.

LAERTES: Where is my father?

KING: Dead.

QUEEN: But not by him.

KING: Let him demand his fill.

LAERTES: How came he dead? I'll not be juggled with:
To hell, allegiance! vows, to the blackest devil!
Conscience and grace, to the profoundest pit!
I dare damnation. To this point I stand,
That both the worlds I give to negligence,
Let come what comes; only I'll be revenged
Most thoroughly for my father.

KING: Who shall stay you?

LAERTES: My will, not all the world:
And for my means, I'll husband them so well,
They shall go far with little.

KING: Good Laertes,
If you desire to know the certainty
Of your dear father's death, is't writ in your revenge,
That, swoopstake, you will draw both friend and foe,
Winner and loser?

LAERTES: None but his enemies.

KING: Will you know them then?

LAERTES: To his good friends thus wide I'll ope my arms;
And like the kind life-rendering pelican,
Repast them with my blood.
KING: Why, now you speak
Like a good child and a true gentleman.
That I am guiltless of your father's death,
And am most sensible in grief for it,
It shall as level to your judgment pierce
As day does to your eye.

A noise within. Let her come in.

LAERTES: How now! what noise is that?

Enter Ophelia

O heat, dry up my brains! tears seven times salt,
Burn out the sense and virtue of mine eye!
By heaven, thy madness shall be paid by weight,
Till our scale turn the beam. O rose of May!
Dear maid, kind sister, sweet Ophelia!
O heavens! is't possible, a young maid's wits
Should be as moral as an old man's life?
Nature is fine in love, and where 'tis fine,
It sends some precious instance of itself
After the thing it loves.
OPHELIA: [Sings]
They bore him barefaced on the bier;
Hey non nonny, nonny, hey nonny;
And in his grave rain'd many a tear:

Fare you well, my dove!

LAERTES: Hadst thou thy wits, and didst persuade revenge,
It could not move thus.

OPHELIA: You must sing a-down a-down,
And you call him a-down-a.
O, how the wheel becomes it! It is the false steward,
That stole his master's daughter.

LAERTES: This nothing's more than matter.

OPHELIA: There's rosemary, that's for remembrance; pray, love, remember: and there is pansies. that's for thoughts.

LAERTES: A document in madness, thoughts and remembrance fitted.

OPHELIA: There's fennel for you, and columbines: there's rue for you; and here's some for me: we may call it herb-grace a' Sundays: O you must wear your rue with a difference. There's a daisy: I would give you some violets, but they withered all when my father died: they say he made a good end.
For bonny sweet Robin is all my joy.

LAERTES: Thought and affliction, passion, hell itself,
She turns to favour and to prettiness.

OPHELIA: [Sings]

And will he not come again,
And will he not come again?
No, no, he is dead:
Go to thy death-bed:

He never will come again.
His beard was as white as snow,
All flaxen was his poll:
He is gone, he is gone,
And we cast away moan:
God ha' mercy on his soul!
And of all Christian souls, I pray God. God be wi' ye.

Exeunt

LAERTES: Do you see this, O God?

KING: Laertes, I must commune with your grief,
Or you deny me right. Go but apart,
Make choice of whom your wisest friends you will.
And they shall hear and judge 'twixt you and me:
If by direct or by collateral hand
They find us touch'd, we will our kingdom give,
Our crown, our life, and all that we call ours,
To you in satisfaction; but if not,
Be you content to lend your patience to us,
And we shall jointly labour with your soul
To give it due content.

LAERTES: Let this be so;
His means of death, his obscure funeral
No trophy, sword, nor hatchment o'er his bones,
No noble rite nor formal ostentation
Cry to be heard, as 'twere from heaven to earth,
That I must call't in question.

KING: So you shall;
And where the offence is, let the great axe fall.
I pray you, go with me.

Exeunt

IV. 6

Enter Horatio and a Servant

HORATIO: What are they that would speak with me?

SERVANT: Sailors, sir: they say they have letters for you.

HORATIO: Let them come in.
I do not know from what part of the world
I should be greeted, if not from Lord Hamlet.

Enter Sailors

SAILOR: God bless you, sir.

HORATIO: Let him bless thee too.

SAILOR: He shall, sir, an't please him. There's a letter for you, sir; it comes from the ambassador that was bound for England; if your name be Horatio, as I am let to know it is.

HORATIO: [Reads the letter] *'Horatio, when thou shalt have over looked this, give these fellows some means to the king: they have letters for him. Ere we were two days old at sea, a pirate of very warlike appointment gave us chase. Finding ourselves too slow of sail, we put on a compelled valour, and in the grapple I boarded them: on the instant they got clear of our ship; so I alone became their prisoner. They have dealt with me like thieves of mercy: but they knew what they did; I am to do a good turn for them. Let the King have the letters I have sent; and repair thou to me with as much speed as thou wouldst fly death. I have words to speak in thine ear, will make thee dumb; yet are they much too light for the bore of the matter. These good fellows will bring thee where I am. Rosencrantz and Guildenstern hold their course for England: of them I have much to tell thee. Farewell.*

'He that thou knowest thine. Hamlet.

Come, I will make you way for these your letters;
And do't the speedier, that you may direct me
To him from whom you brought them.

Exeunt

IV. 7

Enter King Claudius and Laertes

KING: Now must your conscience my acquaintance seal,
And you must put me in your heart for friend,
Sith you have heard, and with a knowing ear,
That he which hath your noble father slain,
Pursued my life.

LAERTES: It well appears: but tell me
Why you proceeded not against these feats,
So crimeful and so capital in nature,
As by your safety, wisdom, all things else,
You mainly were stirr'd up.

KING: O, for two special reasons;
Which may to you, perhaps, seem much unsinew'd,
But yet to me they are strong. The Queen his mother
Lives almost by his looks; and for myself
My virtue or my plague, be it either which
She's so conjunctive to my life and soul,
That, as the star moves not but in his sphere,
I could not but by her. The other motive,
Why to a public count I might not go,
Is the great love the general gender bear him;
Who, dipping all his faults in their affection,
Would, like the spring that turneth wood to stone,
Convert his gyves to graces; so that my arrows,
Too slightly timber'd for so loud a wind,
Would have reverted to my bow again,
And not where I had aim'd them.

LAERTES: And so have I a noble father lost;
A sister driven into desperate terms,
Whose worth, if praises may go back again,
Stood challenger on mount of all the age
For her perfections: but my revenge will come.

KING: Break not your sleeps for that: you must not think
That we are made of stuff so flat and dull
That we can let our beard be shook with danger
And think it pastime. You shortly shall hear more:
I loved your father, and we love ourself;

And that, I hope, will teach you to imagine

Enter a Messenger

How now! what news?

MESSENGER: Letters, my Lord, from Hamlet:
This to your majesty; this to the queen.

KING: From Hamlet! who brought them?

MESSENGER: Sailors, my lord, they say; I saw them not:
They were given me by Claudio; he received them
Of him that brought them.

KING: Laertes, you shall hear them. Leave us.

Exit Messenger

[Reads] *'High and mighty, You shall know I am set naked on your kingdom. To-morrow shall I beg leave to see your kingly eyes: when I shall, first asking your pardon thereunto, recount the occasion of my sudden and more strange return.* Hamlet.

What should this mean? Are all the rest come back?
Or is it some abuse, and no such thing?

LAERTES: Know you the hand?

KING: 'Tis Hamlet's character. Naked!
And in a postscript here, he says 'alone.'
Can you advise me?

LAERTES: I'm lost in it, my Lord. But let him come;
It warms the very sickness in my heart,
That I shall live and tell him to his teeth,
'Thus didest thou.'

KING: If it be so, Laertes

As how should it be so, how otherwise?
Will you be ruled by me?
LAERTES: Ay, my Lord;
So you will not o'errule me to a peace.
KING: To thine own peace. If he be now return'd,
As checking at his voyage, and that he means
No more to undertake it, I will work him
To an exploit, now ripe in my device,
Under the which he shall not choose but fall:
And for his death no wind of blame shall breathe,
But even his mother shall uncharge the practice
And call it accident.
LAERTES: My Lord, I will be ruled;
The rather, if you could devise it so
That I might be the organ.
KING: It falls right.
You have been talk'd of since your travel much,
And that in Hamlet's hearing, for a quality
Wherein, they say, you shine: your sum of parts
Did not together pluck such envy from him
As did that one, and that, in my regard,
Of the unworthiest siege.
LAERTES: What part is that, my Lord?
KING: A very riband in the cap of youth,
Yet needful too; for youth no less becomes
The light and careless livery that it wears

Than settled age his sables and his weeds,
Importing health and graveness. Two months since,
Here was a gentleman of Normandy:
I've seen myself, and served against, the French,
And they can well on horseback: but this gallant
Had witchcraft in't; he grew unto his seat;
And to such wondrous doing brought his horse,
As he had been incorpsed and demi-natur'd
With the brave beast: so far he pass'd my thought,
That I, in forgery of shapes and tricks,
Come short of what he did.

LAERTES: A Norman was't?

KING: A Norman.

LAERTES: Upon my life, Lamond.

KING: The very same.

LAERTES: I know him well: he is the brooch indeed
And gem of all the nation.

KING: He made confession of you,
And gave you such a masterly report
For art and exercise in your defence,
And for your rapier most especially,
That he cried out, 'twould be a sight indeed,
If one could match you: the scrimers of their nation,
He swore, had neither motion, guard nor eye,
If you opposed them. Sir, this report of his
Did Hamlet so envenom with his envy

That he could nothing do but wish and beg
Your sudden coming o'er, to play with him.
Now, out of this,

LAERTES: What out of this, my Lord?

KING: Laertes, was your father dear to you?
Or are you like the painting of a sorrow,
A face without a heart?

LAERTES: Why ask you this?

KING: Not that I think you did not love your father;
But that I know love is begun by Time;
And that I see, in passages of proof,
Time qualifies the spark and fire of it.
There lives within the very flame of love
A kind of wick or snuff that will abate it;
And nothing is at a like goodness still;
For goodness, growing to a plurisy,
Dies in his own too much: that we would do
We should do when we would; for this 'would' changes
And hath abatements and delays as many,
As there are tongues, are hands, are accidents;
And then this 'should' is like a spendthrift sigh,
That hurts by easing. But, to the quick o' the ulcer:
Hamlet comes back: what would you undertake,
To show yourself your father's son indeed
More than in words?

LAERTES: To cut his throat i' th' church.

KING: No place, indeed, should murder sanctuarize;
Revenge should have no bounds. But, good Laertes,
Will you do this, keep close within your chamber.
Hamlet return'd, shall know you are come home:
We'll put on those shall praise your excellence
And set a double varnish on the fame
The Frenchman gave you, bring you in fine together
And wager on your heads: he, being remiss,
Most generous and free from all contriving,
Will not peruse the foils; so that, with ease,
Or with a little shuffling, you may choose
A sword unbated, and in a pass of practice
Requite him for your father.

LAERTES: I will do't:
And, for that purpose, I'll anoint my sword.
I bought an unction of a mountebank,
So mortal that, but dip a knife in it,
Where it draws blood, no cataplasm so rare,
Collected from all simples that have virtue
Under the moon, can save the thing from death
That is but scratch'd withal: I'll touch my point
With this contagion, that, if I gall him slightly,
It may be death.

KING: Let's further think of this;
Weigh what convenience both of time and means
May fit us to our shape: if this should fail,

And that our drift look through our bad performance,
'Twere better not assay'd: therefore this project
Should have a back or second, that might hold,
If this should blast in proof. Soft! let me see:
We'll make a solemn wager on your cunnings: I ha't.
When in your motion you are hot and dry
As make your bouts more violent to that end
And that he calls for drink, I'll have prepar'd him
A chalice for the nonce, whereon but sipping,
If he by chance escape your venom'd stuck,
Our purpose may hold there.

Enter Queen Gertrude

How now, sweet queen!

QUEEN: One woe doth tread upon another's heel,
So fast they follow; your sister's drown'd, Laertes.

LAERTES: Drown'd! O, where?

QUEEN: There is a willow grows aslant a brook,
That shows his hoar leaves in the glassy stream;
There with fantastic garlands did she come
Of crow-flowers, nettles, daisies, and long purples
That liberal shepherds give a grosser name,
But our cold maids do dead men's fingers call them:
There, on the pendent boughs her coronet weeds
Clambering to hang, an envious sliver broke;
When down her weedy trophies and herself
Fell in the weeping brook. Her clothes spread wide;

And, mermaid-like, awhile they bore her up:
Which time she chanted snatches of old tunes;
As one incapable of her own distress,
Or like a creature native and indued
Unto that element: but long it could not be
Till that her garments, heavy with their drink,
Pull'd the poor wretch from her melodious lay
To muddy death.

LAERTES: Alas, then, she is drown'd?

QUEEN: Drown'd, drown'd.

LAERTES: Too much of water hast thou, poor Ophelia,
And therefore I forbid my tears: but yet
It is our trick; nature her custom holds,
Let shame say what it will: when these are gone,
The woman will be out. Adieu, my Lord:
I have a speech of fire, that fain would blaze,
But that this folly douts it.

Exit

KING: Let's follow, Gertrude:
How much I had to do to calm his rage!
Now fear I this will give it start again;
Therefore let's follow.

Exeunt

V. 1

Enter two Clowns.

FIRST CLOWN: Is she to be buried in Christian burial that wilfully seeks her own salvation?

SECOND CLOWN: I tell thee she is: and therefore make her grave straight: the crowner hath sat on her, and finds it Christian burial.

FIRST CLOWN: How can that be, unless she drowned herself in her own defence?

SECOND CLOWN: Why, 'tis found so.

FIRST CLOWN: It must be '*se offendendo;*' it cannot be else. For here lies the point: if I drown myself wittingly, it argues an act: and an act hath three branches: it is, to act, to do, to perform: argal, she drowned herself wittingly.

SECOND CLOWN: Nay, but hear you, goodman delver,

FIRST CLOWN: Give me leave. Here lies the water; good: here stands the man; good; if the man go to this water, and drown himself, it is, will he, nill he, he goes, mark you that; but if the water come to him and drown him, he drowns not himself: argal, he that is not guilty of his own death shortens not his own life.

SECOND CLOWN: But is this law?

FIRST CLOWN: Ay, marry, is't; crowner's Quest Law.

SECOND CLOWN: Will you ha' the truth on't? If this had not been a gentlewoman, she should have been buried out o' Christian burial.

FIRST CLOWN: Why, there thou say'st: and the more pity

that great folk should have countenance in this world to drown or hang themselves, more than their even Christian. Come, my spade. There is no ancient gentleman but gardeners, ditchers, and grave-makers: they hold up Adam's profession.

SECOND CLOWN: Was he a gentleman?

FIRST CLOWN: He was the first that ever bore arms.

SECOND CLOWN: Why, he had none.

FIRST CLOWN: What, art a heathen? How dost thou understand the Scripture? The Scripture says 'Adam digged:' could he dig without arms? I'll put another question to thee: if thou answerest me not to the purpose, confess thyself.

SECOND CLOWN: Go to.

FIRST CLOWN: What is he that builds stronger than either the mason, the shipwright, or the carpenter?

SECOND CLOWN: The gallows-maker; for that frame outlives a thousand tenants.

FIRST CLOWN: I like thy wit well, in good faith: the gallows does well; but how does it well? it does well to those that do ill: now thou dost ill to say the gallows is built stronger than the church: argal, the gallows may do well to thee. To't again, come.

SECOND CLOWN: 'Who builds stronger than a mason, a shipwright, or a carpenter?'

FIRST CLOWN: Ay, tell me that, and unyoke.

SECOND CLOWN: Marry, now I can tell.

FIRST CLOWN: To't.

SECOND CLOWN: Mass, I cannot tell.

Enter Hamlet and Horatio, at a distance

FIRST CLOWN: Cudgel thy brains no more about it, for your dull ass will not mend his pace with beating; and, when you are asked this question next, say a grave-maker: the houses that he makes, last till Doomsday. Go, get thee to Yaughan: fetch me a stoup of liquor.

Exit Second Clown

He digs and sings

In youth, when I did love, did love,
Methought it was very sweet,
To contract, O, the time, for, ah, my behove,
O, methought, there was nothing meet.

HAMLET: Has this fellow no feeling of his business, that he sings at grave-making?

HORATIO: Custom hath made it in him a property of easiness.

HAMLET: 'Tis e'en so: the hand of little employment hath the daintier sense.

FIRST CLOWN: Sings

But age, with his stealing steps,
Hath claw'd me in his clutch,
And hath shipped me intil the land,
As if I had never been such.

Throws up a skull

HAMLET: That skull had a tongue in it, and could sing

once: how the knave jowls it to the ground, as if it were Cain's jaw-bone, that did the first murder! It might be the pate of a politician, which this ass now o'er-reaches; one that would circumvent God, might it not?

HORATIO: It might, my Lord.

HAMLET: Or of a courtier; which could say 'Good morrow, sweet lord! How dost thou, good Lord?' This might be my lord such-a-one, that praised my Lord such-a-one's horse, when he meant to beg it; might it not?

HORATIO: Ay, my Lord.

HAMLET: Why, e'en so: and now my Lady Worm's; chapless, and knocked about the mazzard with a sexton's spade: here's fine revolution, if we had the trick to see't. Did these bones cost no more the breeding, but to play at loggats with 'em? mine ache to think on't.

FIRST CLOWN: Sings

A pick-axe, and a spade, a spade,
For and a shrouding sheet:
O, a pit of clay for to be made
For such a guest is meet.

Throws up another skull.

HAMLET: There's another: why may not that be the skull of a lawyer? Where be his quiddities now, his quillets, his cases, his tenures, and his tricks? why does he suffer this rude knave now to knock him about the sconce with a dirty shovel, and will not tell him of his action of battery? Hum! This fellow might be in's time a great buyer of land, with his statutes, his recognizances, his fines, his double vouchers, his recoveries: is this the fine of his fines, and the recovery of his recoveries, to have his fine pate full of fine dirt? will his vouchers vouch him no more of his purchases, and double ones too, than the length and breadth of a pair of indentures? The very conveyances of his lands will hardly lie in this box; and must the inheritor himself have no more, ha?

HORATIO: Not a jot more, my Lord.

HAMLET: Is not parchment made of sheep-skins?

HORATIO: Ay, my Lord, and of calf-skins too.

HAMLET: They are sheep and calves which seek out assurance in that. I will speak to this fellow. Whose grave's this, sirrah?

FIRST CLOWN: Mine, sir.

O, a pit of clay for to be made
For such a guest is meet.

HAMLET: I think it be thine, indeed; for thou liest in't.

FIRST CLOWN: You lie out on't, sir, and therefore it is not yours: for my part, I do not lie in't, and yet it is mine.

HAMLET: 'Thou dost lie in't, to be in't and say it is thine: 'tis for the dead, not for the quick; therefore thou liest.

FIRST CLOWN: 'Tis a quick lie, sir; 'twill away gain, from me to you.

HAMLET: What man dost thou dig it for?

FIRST CLOWN: For no man, sir.

HAMLET: What woman, then?

FIRST CLOWN: For none, neither.

HAMLET: Who is to be buried in't?

FIRST CLOWN: One that was a woman, sir; but, rest her soul, she's dead.

HAMLET: How absolute the knave is! we must speak by the card, or equivocation will undo us. By the Lord, Horatio, these three years I have taken a note of it; the age is grown so picked that the toe of the peasant comes so near the heel of the courtier, he gaffs his kibe. How long hast thou been a grave-maker?

FIRST CLOWN: Of all the days i' th' year, I came to't that day that our last king Hamlet overcame Fortinbras.

HAMLET: How long is that since?

FIRST CLOWN: Cannot you tell that? every fool can tell that: it was the very day that young Hamlet was born; he that is mad, and sent into England.

HAMLET: Ay, marry, why was he sent into England?

FIRST CLOWN: Why, because he was mad: he shall recover his wits there; or, if he do not, it's no great matter there.

HAMLET: Why?

FIRST CLOWN: 'Twill not be seen in him there; there the men are as mad as he.

HAMLET: How came he mad?

FIRST CLOWN: Very strangely, they say.

HAMLET: How strangely?

FIRST CLOWN: Faith, e'en with losing his wits.

HAMLET: Upon what ground?

FIRST CLOWN: Why, here in Denmark: I have been sexton here, man and boy, thirty years.

HAMLET: How long will a man lie i' th' earth ere he rot?

FIRST CLOWN: I' faith, if he be not rotten before he die— as we have many pocky corses now-a-days, that will scarce hold the laying in—he will last you some eight year or nine year: a tanner will last you nine year.

HAMLET: Why he more than another?

FIRST CLOWN: Why, sir, his hide is so tanned with his trade, that he will keep out water a great while; and your water is a sore decayer of your whoreson dead body. Here's a skull now; this skull has lain in the earth three and twenty years.

HAMLET: Whose was it?

FIRST CLOWN: A whoreson mad fellow's it was: whose do you think it was?

HAMLET: Nay, I know not.

FIRST CLOWN: A pestilence on him for a mad rogue! a' pour'd a flagon of Rhenish on my head once. This same skull, sir, was Yorick's skull, the King's jester.

HAMLET: This?

FIRST CLOWN: E'en that.

HAMLET: Let me see.

(Takes the skull)

Alas, poor Yorick! I knew him, Horatio: a fellow of infinite jest, of most excellent fancy: he hath borne me on his back a thousand times; and now, how abhorred in my imagination it is! my gorge rises at it. Here hung those lips that I have kissed I know not how oft. Where be your gibes now? your gambols? your songs? your flashes of merriment, that were wont to set the table on a roar? Not one now, to mock your own grinning? quite chop-fallen? Now get you to my lady's chamber, and tell her, let her paint an inch thick, to this favour she must come; make her laugh at that. Prithee, Horatio, tell me one thing.

HORATIO: What's that, my Lord?

HAMLET: Dost thou think Alexander looked o' this fashion i' th' earth?

HORATIO: E'en so.

HAMLET: And smelt so? puh!

HORATIO: E'en so, my Lord.

HAMLET: To what base uses we may return, Horatio! Why may not imagination trace the noble dust of Alexander, till he find it stopping a bung-hole?

HORATIO: 'Twere to consider too curiously, to consider so.

HAMLET: No, faith, not a jot; but to follow him thither with modesty enough, and likelihood to lead it: as thus: Alexander died, Alexander was buried, Alexander returneth into dust; the dust is earth; of earth we make loam; and why of that loam, whereto he was converted, might they not stop a beer-barrel?

Imperious Caesar, dead and turn'd to clay,
Might stop a hole to keep the wind away:
O, that that earth, which kept the world in awe,
Should patch a wall to expel the winter flaw!
But soft! but soft! aside: here comes the king.

Enter bearers with a coffin, the King and Queen, Laertes and other Lords, a Priest following.

The Queen, the courtiers: who is this they follow?
And with such maimed rites? This doth betoken
The corse they follow did with desperate hand,
Fordo its own life: 'twas of some estate.
Couch we awhile, and mark.

LAERTES: What ceremony else?

HAMLET: That is Laertes,
A very noble youth: mark.

LAERTES: What ceremony else?

PRIEST: Her obsequies have been as far enlarg'd
As we have warrantise: her death was doubtful;
And, but that great command o'ersways the order,
She should in ground unsanctified have lodged
Till the last trumpet: for charitable prayers,
Shards, flints and pebbles should be thrown on her;
Yet here she is allow'd her virgin rites,
Her maiden strewments and the bringing home
Of bell and burial.

LAERTES: Must there no more be done?

PRIEST: No more be done:
We should profane the service of the dead
To sing a requiem and such rest to her
As to peace-parted souls.
LAERTES: Lay her i' th' earth:
And from her fair and unpolluted flesh
May violets spring! I tell thee, churlish priest,
A ministering angel shall my sister be,
When thou liest howling.
HAMLET: What, the fair Ophelia!
QUEEN: Sweets to the sweet: farewell!
I hoped thou shouldst have been my Hamlet's wife;
I thought thy bride-bed to have deck'd, sweet maid,
And not have strew'd thy grave.
LAERTES: O, treble woe,
Fall ten times treble on that cursed head,
Whose wicked deed thy most ingenious sense
Deprived thee of! Hold off the earth awhile,
Till I have caught her once more in mine arms:

Leaps into the grave

Now pile your dust upon the quick and dead,
Till of this flat a mountain you have made,
To o'ertop old Pelion, or the skyish head
Of blue Olympus.
HAMLET: What is he, whose griefs
Bears such an emphasis? whose phrase of sorrow

Conjures the wandering stars, and makes them stand
Like wonder-wounded hearers? This is I,
Hamlet the Dane.

Hamlet leaps into the grave

LAERTES: The devil take thy soul!

HAMLET: Thou pray'st not well.
I prithee, take thy fingers from my throat;
For, though I am not splenitive and rash,
Yet have I something in me dangerous,
Which let thy wiseness fear: hold off thy hand.

KING: Pluck them asunder.

QUEEN: Hamlet, Hamlet!

HORATIO: Good my Lord, be quiet.

HAMLET: Why I will fight with him upon this theme
Until my eyelids will no longer wag.

QUEEN: O my son, what theme?

HAMLET: I loved Ophelia: forty thousand brothers
Could not, with all their quantity of love,
Make up my sum. What wilt thou do for her?

KING: O, he is mad, Laertes.

QUEEN: For love of God, forbear him.

HAMLET: Come show me what thou'lt do:
Woo't weep? woo't fight? woo't fast? woo't tear thyself?
Woo't drink up eisel, eat a crocodile?
I'll do't. Dost thou come here to whine?

To outface me with leaping in her grave?
Be buried quick with her, and so will I:
And, if thou prate of mountains, let them throw
Millions of acres on us, till our ground,
Singeing his pate against the burning zone,
Make Ossa like a wart! Nay, an thou'lt mouth,
I'll rant as well as thou.

QUEEN: This is mere madness:
And thus awhile the fit will work on him;
Anon, as patient as the female dove,
When that her golden couplets are disclosed,
His silence will sit drooping.

HAMLET: Hear you, sir;
What is the reason that you use me thus?
I loved you ever: but it is no matter;
Let Hercules himself do what he may,
The cat will mew and dog will have his day.

Exeunt

KING: I pray you, good Horatio, wait upon him.

Exit Horatio

Strengthen your patience in our last night's speech;
We'll put the matter to the present push.
Good Gertrude, set some watch over your son.
This grave shall have a living monument:
An hour of quiet shortly shall we see;
Till then, in patience our proceeding be.

Exeunt

V. 2

Enter Hamlet and Horatio

HAMLET: So much for this, sir: now shall you see the other;
You do remember all the circumstance?
HORATIO: Remember it, my Lord?
HAMLET: Sir, in my heart there was a kind of fighting,
That would not let me sleep: methought I lay
Worse than the mutines in the bilboes. Rashly,
And praised be rashness for it, let us know,
Our indiscretion sometimes serves us well,
When our deep plots do pall: and that should teach us,
There's a divinity that shapes our ends,
Rough-hew them how we will,
HORATIO: That is most certain.
HAMLET: Up from my cabin,
My sea-gown scarf'd about me, in the dark
Groped I to find out them; had my desire.
Finger'd their packet, and in fine withdrew
To mine own room again; making so bold,
My fears forgetting manners, to unseal
Their grand commission; where I found Horatio,
O royal knavery! an exact command,
Larded with many several sorts of reasons,
Importing Denmark's health and England's too,
With, hoo! such bugs and goblins in my life,
That, on the supervise, no leisure bated,

No, not to stay the grinding of the axe,
My head should be struck off.
HORATIO: Is't possible?
HAMLET: Here's the commission: read it at more leisure.
But wilt thou hear me how I did proceed?
HORATIO: I beseech you.
HAMLET: Being thus be-netted round with villanies,
Or I could make a prologue to my brains,
They had begun the play I sat me down,
Devis'd a new commission, wrote it fair:
I once did hold it, as our statists do,
A baseness to write fair and labour'd much
How to forget that learning, but, sir, now
It did me yeoman's service: wilt thou know
The effect of what I wrote?
HORATIO: Ay, good my Lord.
HAMLET: An earnest conjuration from the King,
As England was his faithful tributary,
As love between them like the palm might flourish,
As peace should stiff her wheaten garland wear
And stand a comma 'tween their amities,
And many such-like As'es of great charge,
That, on the view and knowing of these contents,
Without debatement further, more or less,
He should the bearers put to sudden death,
Not shriving-time allow'd.

HORATIO: How was this seal'd?

HAMLET: Why, even in that was heaven ordinate.
I had my father's signet in my purse,
Which was the model of that Danish seal;
Folded the writ up in form of the other,
Subscribed it, gave't the impression, placed it safely,
The changeling never known. Now, the next day
Was our sea-fight; and what to this was sequent
Thou know'st already.

HORATIO: So Guildenstern and Rosencrantz go to't.

HAMLET: Why, man, they did make love to this employment;
They are not near my conscience; their defeat
Doth by their own insinuation grow:
'Tis dangerous when the baser nature comes
Between the pass and fell incensed points
Of mighty opposites.

KORATIO: Why, what a King is this!

HAMLET: Does it not, think'st thee, stand me now upon
He that hath kill'd my King and whor'd my mother,
Popp'd in between the election and my hopes,
Thrown out his angle for my proper life,
And with such cozenage is't not perfect conscience,
To quit him with this arm? and is't not to be damn'd,
To let this canker of our nature come
In further evil?

HORATIO: It must be shortly known to him from England
What is the issue of the business there.
HAMLET: It will be short: the interim is mine;
And a man's life's no more than to say 'One.'
But I am very sorry, good Horatio,
That to Laertes I forgot myself;
For, by the image of my cause, I see
The portraiture of his: I'll court his favours.
But, sure, the bravery of his grief did put me
Into a towering passion.
HORATIO: Peace! who comes here?

Enter Osric

OSRIC: Your lordship is right welcome back to Denmark.

HAMLET: I humbly thank you, sir. Dost know this water-fly?

HORATIO: No, my good Lord.

HAMLET: Thy state is the more gracious; for 'tis a vice to know him. He hath much land, and fertile: let a beast be lord of beasts, and his crib shall stand at the king's mess: 'tis a chough; but, as I say, spacious in the possession of dirt.

OSRIC: Sweet Lord, if your lordship were at leisure, I should impart a thing to you from his majesty.

HAMLET: I will receive it, sir, with all diligence of spirit. Put your bonnet to his right use; 'tis for the head.

OSRIC: I thank your Lordship, it is very hot.

HAMLET: No, believe me, 'tis very cold; the wind is northerly.

OSRIC: It is indifferent cold, my Lord, indeed.

HAMLET: But yet methinks it is very sultry and hot for my complexion.

OSRIC: Exceedingly, my Lord; it is very sultry,—as 'twere, I cannot tell how. But, my lord, his majesty bade me signify to you that he has laid a great wager on your head: sir, this is the matter,

HAMLET: I beseech you, remember.

OSRIC: Nay, good my lord; for mine ease, in good faith. Sir, here is newly come to court Laertes; believe me, an absolute gentleman, full of most excellent differences, of very soft society and great showing: indeed, to speak feelingly of him, he is the card or calendar of gentry, for you shall find in him the continent of what part a gentleman would see.

HAMLET: Sir, his definement suffers no perdition in you; though, I know, to divide him inventorially would dizzy the arithmetic of memory, and yet but yaw neither, in respect of his quick sail. But, in the verity of extolment, I take him to be a soul of great article; and his infusion of such dearth and rareness, as, to make true diction of him, his semblable is his mirror; and who else would trace him, his umbrage, nothing more.

OSRIC: Your Lordship speaks most infallibly of him.

HAMLET: The concernancy, sir, why do we wrap the gentleman in our more rawer breath?

OSRIC: Sir?

HORATIO: Is't not possible to understand in another tongue?

You will do't, sir, really.

HAMLET: What imports the nomination of this gentleman?

OSRIC: Of Laertes?

HORATIO: His purse is empty already; all's golden words are spent.

HAMLET: Of him, sir.

OSRIC: I know you are not ignorant

HAMLET: I would you did, sir; yet, in faith, if you did, it would not much approve me. Well, sir?

OSRIC: You are not ignorant of what excellence Laertes is.

HAMLET: I dare not confess that, lest I should compare with him in excellence; but, to know a man well, were to know himself.

OSRIC: I mean, sir, for his weapon; but in the imputation laid on him by them, in his meed he's unfellowed.

HAMLET: What's his weapon?

OSRIC: Rapier and dagger.

HAMLET: That's two of his weapons: but, well.

OSRIC: The King, sir, hath wagered with him six Barbary horses: against the which he has imponed, as I take it, six French rapiers and poniards, with their assigns, as girdle, hangers, and so: three of the carriages, in faith, are very dear to fancy, very responsive to the hilts, most delicate carriages, and of very liberal conceit.

HAMLET: What call you the carriages?

HORATIO: I knew you must be edified by the margent ere you had done.

OSRIC: The carriages, sir, are the hangers.

HAMLET: The phrase would be more germane to the matter, if we could carry cannon by our sides: I would it might be hangers till then. But, on: six Barbary horses against six French swords, their assigns, and three liberal-conceited carriages; that's the French bet against the Danish. Why is this 'imponed,' as you call it?

OSRIC: The King, sir, hath laid, that in a dozen passes between yourself and him, he shall not exceed you three hits: he hath laid on twelve for nine; and it would come to immediate trial, if your lordship would vouchsafe the answer.

HAMLET: How if I answer 'no'?

OSRIC: I mean, my Lord, the opposition of your person in trial.

HAMLET: Sir, I will walk here in the hall: if it please his majesty, 'tis the breathing time of day with me; let the foils be brought, the gentleman willing, and the King hold his purpose, I will win for him if I can; if not, I will gain nothing but my shame and the odd hits.

OSRIC: Shall I re-deliver you e'en so?

HAMLET: To this effect, sir; after what flourish your

nature will.

OSRIC: I commend my duty to your lordship.

HAMLET: Yours, yours.

Exit Osric

He does well to commend it himself; there are no tongues else for's turn.

HORATIO: This lapwing runs away with the shell on his head.

HAMLET: He did comply with his dug, before he sucked it. Thus has he—and many more of the same bevy that I know the dressy age dotes on—only got the tune of the time and outward habit of encounter; a kind of yesty collection, which carries them through and through the most fond and winnowed opinions; and do but blow them to their trial, the bubbles are out.

Enter a Lord

LORD: My Lord, his majesty commended him to you by young Osric, who brings back to him that you attend him in the Hall: he sends to know if your pleasure hold to play with Laertes, or that you will take longer time.

HAMLET: I am constant to my purpose; they follow the King's pleasure: if his fitness speaks, mine is ready; now or whensoever, provided I be so able as now.

LORD: The King and Queen and all are coming down.

HAMLET: In happy time.

LORD: The Queen desires you to use some gentle entertainment to Laertes before you fall to play.

HAMLET: She well instructs me.

Exit Lord

HORATIO: You will lose this wager, my Lord.

HAMLET: I do not think so: since he went into France, I have been in continual practice: I shall win at the odds. But thou wouldst not think how ill all's here about my heart: but it is no matter.

HORATIO: Nay, good my Lord.

HAMLET: It is but foolery; but it is such a kind of gain-giving, as would perhaps trouble a woman.

HORATIO: If your mind dislike any thing, obey it: I will forestall their repair hither, and say you are not fit.

HAMLET: Not a whit, we defy augury: there's a special providence in the fall of a sparrow. If it be now, 'tis not to come; if it be not to come, it will be now; if it be not now, yet it will come: the readiness is all: since no man has aught of what he leaves, what is't to leave betimes?

Enter King Claudius, Queen Gertrude, Laertes, Lords, Osric, and Attendants with foils, and daggers

KING: Come, Hamlet, come, and take this hand from me.

HAMLET: Give me your pardon, sir: I've done you wrong;
But pardon't, as you are a gentleman.
This presence knows,
And you must needs have heard, how I am punish'd
With sore distraction. What I have done,
That might your nature, honour and exception

Roughly awake, I here proclaim was madness.
Was't Hamlet wrong'd Laertes? Never Hamlet:
If Hamlet from himself be ta'en away,
And when he's not himself does wrong Laertes,
Then Hamlet does it not, Hamlet denies it.
Who does it, then? His madness: if't be so,
Hamlet is of the faction that is wrong'd;
His madness is poor Hamlet's enemy.
Sir, in this audience,
Let my disclaiming from a purpos'd evil
Free me so far in your most generous thoughts,
That I have shot mine arrow o'er the house,
And hurt my brother.

LAERTES: I am satisfied in Nature,
Whose motive, in this case, should stir me most
To my revenge: but in my terms of honour
I stand aloof; and will no reconcilement,
Till by some elder masters, of known honour,
I have a voice and precedent of peace,
To keep my name ungored. But till that time,
I do receive your offer'd love like love,
And will not wrong it.

HAMLET: I embrace it freely;
And will this brother's wager frankly play.
Give us the foils. Come on.

LAERTES: Come, one for me.

HAMLET: I'll be your foil, Laertes: in mine ignorance
Your skill shall, like a star i' th' darkest night,
Stick fiery off indeed.
LAERTES: You mock me, sir.
HAMLET: No, by this hand.
KING: Give them the foils, young Osric. Cousin Hamlet,
You know the wager?
HAMLET: Very well, my Lord
Your grace hath laid the odds o' th' weaker side.
KING: I do not fear it; I have seen you both:
But since he is better'd, we have therefore odds.
LAERTES: This is too heavy, let me see another.
HAMLET: This likes me well. These foils have all a length?

They prepare to play

OSRIC: Ay, my good Lord.
KING: Set me the stoops of wine upon that table.
If Hamlet give the first or second hit,
Or quit in answer of the third exchange,
Let all the battlements their ordnance fire:
The King shall drink to Hamlet's better breath;
And in the cup an union shall he throw,
Richer than that which four successive Kings
In Denmark's crown have worn. Give me the cups;
And let the kettle to the trumpet speak,
The trumpet to the cannoneer without,
The cannons to the heavens, the heavens to earth,

'Now the King drinks to Hamlet.' Come, begin:
And you, the judges, bear a wary eye.

HAMLET: Come on, sir.

LAERTES: Come, my Lord.

They play

HAMLET: One.

LAERTES: No.

HAMLET: Judgment.

OSRIC: A hit, a very palpable hit.

LAERTES: Well; again.

KING: Stay; give me drink. Hamlet, this pearl is thine;
Here's to thy health.
Give him the cup.

Drums, trumpets and shot. Flounish. A piece goes off.

HAMLET: I'll play this bout first; set it by awhile. Come.

They play

Another hit; what say you?

LAERTES: A touch, a touch, I do confess.

KING: Our son shall win.

QUEEN: He's fat, and scant of breath.
Here, Hamlet, take my napkin, rub thy brows;
The Queen carouses to thy fortune, Hamlet.

HAMLET: Good Madam!

KING: Gertrude, do not drink.

QUEEN: I will, my Lord; I pray you, pardon me.

KING: It is the poison'd cup: it is too late.

HAMLET: I dare not drink yet, Madam; by and by.
QUEEN: Come, let me wipe thy face.
LAERTES: My Lord, I'll hit him now.
KING: I do not think't.
LAERTES: And yet 'tis almost 'gainst my conscience.
HAMLET: Come, for the third, Laertes: you but dally;
I pray you, pass with your best violence;
I am afear'd you make a wanton of me.
LAERTES: Say you so? come on.
OSRIC: Nothing, neither way.
LAERTES: Have at you now!

Laertes wounds Hamlet; then in scuffling, they change rapiers, and Hamlet wounds Laertes

KING: Part them; they are incens'd.
HAMLET: Nay, come, again.

Queen Gertrude falls down, dying

OSRIC: Look to the Queen there, ho!
HORATIO: They bleed on both sides. How is it, my Lord?
OSRIC: How is't, Laertes?
LAERTES: Why, as a woodcock to mine own springe, Osric;
I am justly kill'd with mine own treachery.
HAMLET: How does the Queen?
KING: She sounds to see them bleed.
QUEEN: No, no, the drink, the drink, O my dear Hamlet,
The drink, the drink! I am poison'd.

Dies

HAMLET: O villany! Ho! let the door be lock'd:
Treachery! Seek it out.

LAERTES: It is here, Hamlet: Hamlet, thou art slain;
No medicine in the world can do thee good;
In thee there is not half an hour of life;
The treacherous instrument is in thy hand,
Unbated and envenom'd: the foul practice
Hath turn'd itself on me lo, here I lie,
Never to rise again: thy mother's poison'd:
I can no more: the King, the King's to blame.

HAMLET: The point!—envenom'd too!
Then, venom, to thy work.

Stabs the King

ALL: Treason! treason!

KING: O, yet defend me, friends; I am but hurt.

HAMLET: Here, thou incestuous, murderous, damned Dane,
Drink off this potion. Is thy union here?
Follow my mother.

King Claudius dies

LAERTES: He is justly served;
It is a poison temper'd by himself.
Exchange forgiveness with me, noble Hamlet:
Mine and my father's death come not upon thee,
Nor thine on me.

HAMLET: Heaven make thee free of it! I follow thee.
I am dead, Horatio. Wretched queen, adieu!
You that look pale and tremble at this chance,
That are but mutes or audience to this act,
Had I but time as this fell sergeant, death,
Is strict in his arrest O, I could tell you
But let it be. Horatio, I am dead;
Thou liv'st; report me and my cause aright
To the unsatisfied.

HORATIO: Never believe it:
I am more an antique Roman than a Dane:
Here's yet some liquor left.

HAMLET: As thou'rt a man,
Give me the cup: let go; by heaven, I'll have't.
O good Horatio, what a wounded name,
Things standing thus unknown, shall live behind me!
If thou didst ever hold me in thy heart
Absent thee from felicity awhile,
And in this harsh world draw thy breath in pain,
To tell my story.

March afar off, and shot within

What warlike noise is this?

OSRIC: Young Fortinbras, with conquest come from Poland,
To the ambassadors of England gives
This warlike volley.

HAMLET: O, I die, Horatio;

The potent poison quite o'er-crows my spirit:
I cannot live to hear the news from England;
But I do prophesy the election lights
On Fortinbras: he has my dying voice;
So tell him, with the occurrents, more and less,
Which have solicited. The rest is silence.

Dies

HORATIO: Now cracks a noble heart. Good night sweet prince:
And flights of angels sing thee to thy rest!
Why does the drum come hither?

Enter Fortinbras, the English Ambassadors, and others

FORTINBRAS: Where is this sight?

HORATIO: What is it ye would see?
If aught of woe or wonder, cease your search.

FORTINBRAS: This quarry cries on havoc. O proud death,
What feast is toward in thine eternal cell,
That thou so many princes at a shot
So bloodily hast struck?

FIRST AMBASSADOR: The sight is dismal;
And our affairs from England come too late:
The ears are senseless that should give us hearing,
To tell him his commandment is fulfill'd,
That Rosencrantz and Guildenstern are dead:
Where should we have our thanks?

HORATIO: Not from his mouth,
Had it the ability of life to thank you:
He never gave commandment for their death.
But since, so jump upon this bloody question,
You from the Polack wars, and you from England,
Are here arrived give order that these bodies
High on a stage be placed to the view;
And let me speak to the yet unknowing world
How these things came about: so shall you hear
Of carnal, bloody, and unnatural acts,
Of accidental judgments, casual slaughters,
Of deaths put on by cunning and forc'd cause,
And, in this upshot, purposes mistook
Fall'n on the inventors' heads: all this can I
Truly deliver.

FORTINBRAS: Let us haste to hear it,
And call the noblest to the audience.
For me, with sorrow I embrace my fortune:
I have some rights of memory in this kingdom,
Which now to claim my vantage doth invite me.

HORATIO: Of that I shall have also cause to speak,
And from his mouth whose voice will draw no more;
But let this same be presently perform'd,
Even while men's minds are wild; lest more mischance
On plots and errors, happen.

FORTINBRAS: Let four captains
Bear Hamlet, like a soldier, to the stage;
For he was likely, had he been put on,
To have proved most royally: and, for his passage,
The soldiers' music and the rites of war
Speak loudly for him.
Take up the body: such a sight as this
Becomes the field, but here shows much amiss.
Go, bid the soldiers shoot.

Exeunt, bearing off the dead bodies; after which a peal of ordnance is shot off

GLOSSARY

abridgement : pastime.
additional : honour.
admiration : wonder, astonishment
aery : nest.
affection : affection.
anchor : anchorite, hermit.
amble : walk affectedly.
angle : rod and line.
annexment : attachment.
antic disposition : pretended madness.
appurtenace : that which belongs to.
argument : plot of a play.
arras : tapestry hanging.
arter : artery.
at point exactly : at all points, complete.
barr'd : thwarted.
bated : abated.
bedded : lying flat.
beetles : just.
beshrew : plague on.
bespeak : command.
beteem : allow.
bisson : blind.
blank : target.
blown youth : youth in full bloom.
bodkin : dagger.
bodykins : little body.
bourne : boundry.
brainish : mad.
braz'd : covered with brass.
breath : utterance.
breathing time : time for exercise.
brokers : go-betweens.
buttons : buds.
buz, buz : stale news.

canon : law.
canopy : covering.
canker : maggot.
cap-a-pe : from head to foot.
capable : capable of feeling.
cataplasm : plaster.
cautel : craft.
censure : opinion.
chaplesss : without cheeks.
character : (a) handwriting.
(b) write.
chough : jackdaw.

clepe : call.
climature : climate, country.
coil : turmoil.
collateral : related, accessory.
comply with : use ceremony with.
compost : manure.
conceit : imagination.
compounded : mixed.
condolement : lamentation.
conjunctive : inseparable.
consequence : sequel.
consummation : conclusion.
continent : able to contain.
contraction : contract of marriage.
convoy : means of conveyance.
coped : encountered.
coted : came alongside.
couch : lie down.
cousin : kinsman.
counter : follow the scent in the wrong direction.
counterfeit presentment : portrait.
crowner : coroner.

Danskers : Danes.
declension : downward path.
discourse of reason : power of reason.
distemper'd : disturbed.
dole : grief.
distilled : melted.
distract : out of her mind.
doublet : short, close-fitting coat.
doubt : suspect.
douts : puts out.
down-gyved : hanging like fetters round his ankles.
drift. of question : indirect inquiry.
drossy : scummy.
dupped : opened.

ecstasy : madness.
effects : material advantages.
eisel : vinegar.
emulate : emulous, jealous.
enactures : resolutions.
encompassments : circumlocution.
encumbered : folded.
entertainment : welcome hospitality.
entreatments : preliminary conversations.
escoted : paid.
espiels : spies.
even : straight.
even Christian : fellow Christian.
extent : outward show.
extorted : evilly acquired.
extravagant : wandering.
eyases : hawks.

faction : party.
fantasy : imagination, illusion.
fardels : burdens.
fat : out of condition.
favuor : face, appearance,
fay : faith.

feats : acts.
fellies : rim of a wheel.
flats : low-lying shore.
flushing : filling with water.
fordo : destroy.
foreknowing : foreknowledge.
forms : mental images.
free : guiltless.
fretted : ornamented.
friending : friendliness.
function : action, behaviour.
fust : grow musty.

gaged : pledged.
gate : bitterness.
gain-giving : misgiving.
gait : progress.
general gender : the people at large.
generous : of gentle birth.
gentry : gentlemanly behaviour.
germane : relative.
gib : tomcat.
God buy : God be with.
God'ild you : God reward you.
gorge : throat.
grizzled : grey.
gross and scope : full view.
gules : red in the jargon of heraldry.
gulf : whirlpool.
gyves : fetters.

habit : garments.
hangers : straps for carrying the sword.
happily : haply.
harrows : distresses.
hearsed : buried.
heat : anger.
hebenon : probably henbane.
hectic : fever.
hic et ubique : here and everywhere.
honest : chaste.
hoodman blind : blind man's buff.
hugger-mugger : 'anyhow', i.e. in secret haste.
husbandry : economy.
Hyperion : the Sun.
Hyrcanian beast : the tiger.

idle : silly.
Ilium : the citadel of Troy.
impasted : encrusted.
imponed : pawned, bet.
imposthume : a boil.
impress : conscription.
incorps'd : of one body with.
incorrect to : unruled by.
inhibition : prohibition.
infants : huds.
instances : motives.
inurned : buried.
investments : outward garments.
it : its.

jig : dance wantonly.
jointress : partner.

journeyman : hired workman.
jowls : claps down.
jump : immediately.
just : exactly.

keep : live.
kettle : kettle drum.
kindless : unnatural.

larded : garnished.
large discourse : power of reasoning.
lazar-like : like leprosy.
lenten : fasting, meagre.
lets : hinders.
liberal conceit : elaborate pattern.
lighted : alighted.
loose : torn loose.
luxury : lust.

made probation : proved to be true.
mazzard : pate.
meed : merit.
merely : utterly.
miching mallecho : slinking mischief.
milch : moist.
mobled : muffled.
moiety competent : adequate share.
mope : be dull.
moth : mote, speck of dust.
mouse : a term of affection.
mows : insulting grimaces.
murdering-pieces : cannon loaded with grape-shot.

nave : centre of a wheel.
nonce : for the once, occasion.

occulted : concealed.
o'erraught : overtook.
o'er-sized : painted over.
o'er-teemed : exhausted by bearing children.
omen : disaster.
operant : active.
opposite : obstacle.
overpeeirng of his list : overstepping its boundary.
outstretched : exaggerated.

paddock : toad.
painted : motionless as in a picture.
painting : imitation.
pajock : peacock.
pales : defences.
pall : fail.
passages of proof : experiences that prove.
performed at height : achieved greatly.
peak : mope
pioner : engineer, or military miner.
plausive : pleasing.
pith : marrow.
plurisy : excess.

policy : state craft.
porpentine : porcupine.
posset : curdle.
powers : forces.
precurse : forerunner.
pregnant : ready, apt.
prenominate : aforesaid.
prescripts : commands.
presently : immediately.
pressure : impression, imprint of a seal.
prevent : forestall.
primy nature : nature in its spring time.
process : procedure.
property of easiness : a matter of indifference.
pursy : puffy.

quaintly : skilfully.
quality : acting profession.
quit : repay.
quoted : noted.

rack : the cloud in the sky.
range : run about.
rank : overgrown.
ranker : richer.
razed : ornamented with cuts.
reach : far sight.
recorder : a wood-wind instrument.
reechy : grimy.
remorse : pity.
replication : echo.
resolve : melt.
respect : consideration.
responsive to : matching well.
retrograde : contrary.
rhapsody : meaningless sound.
rheum : moisture.
riband : ribbon.
rivals : partners.
romage : literally, clearing out the hold of a ship.
rouse : deep draught, carouse.
row : line.

sable : black.
sallets : piquancies.
sanctified : sanctimonious.
saws : wise sayings.
school : university.
scrimers : fencers.
sealed : confirmed the election.
season : (a) qualify, (b) ripen.
secure hour : hour of ease.
seized of : possessed of.
sensible : perceived by the senses.
shark'd up : collected indiscriminately.
sheeted : shrouded.
shent : shoes.
siege : seat, and so rank, importance.
sold in fee : freehold.

sort : (a) fall out, (b) reckon.
sounds : swoons.
splenitive : hot tempered.
springe : snare.
stamp of nature : the impression made by nature : natural character.
station : noble bearing.
statists : statesmen.
still : ever, continuously.
stithy : smithy.
stomach : requiring courage.
stoup : large drinking cup.
stuck : thrust.
subject : subjects.
sullies (spelt *sallies* in the Second Quarto) : blemishes.
suppliance of a minute : momentary.
supposed : estimation.
Switzers : Swiss body-guard.
Swounds : by God's wounds.

taints : blemishes.
takes : bewitches.
tarre on : set on.
lax'd : censured.
temple : i.e. the body.
tempered : mixed.
tend : attend.
tender : (a) offer, (b) counter.
tent : probe.
touch'd : implicated.
tricked : heraldic word for painted.

umbrage : shadow.
unbated : unblunted, sharp.
unction : ointment.
uneffectual : made powerless.
unfortified : irreligious.
ungracious : graceless.
unimproved : unschooled, rash.
union : pearl.
unpregnant : having no living thought within.
unproportioned : unsuitable.
unreclaimed : untouched, naturally wild.
unsifted : untried.
unsinew'd : nerveless.
up-spring : a wild dance.

vailed : lowered.
valanced : fringed, i.e. with a beard.
variable : varied.
varnish : gloss.
ventages : stops in the recorder.
vigour : violent action.
voice : vote.

windlasses : winding about.

yaw : sail unsteadily.
yesty collection : frothy knowledge.

HERITAGE CLASSICS ....

Arms and the Man
Author: *Bernard Shaw*
ISBN: 9788170262312
Price: Rs. 50.00

Down and Out in Paris and London
Author: *George Orwell*
ISBN: 8170262097
Price: Rs. 75.00

The Time Machine
Author: *H. G. Wells*
ISBN: 9788170262343
Price: Rs. 50.00

Burmese Days
Author: *George Orwell*
ISBN: 8170262070
Price: Rs. 75.00

The Old Man and the Sea
Author: *Ernest Hemingway*
ISBN: 9788170262299
Price: Rs. 50.00

Animal Farm
Author: *George Orwell*
ISBN: 8170262089
Price: Rs. 50.00

The Kama Sutra of Vatsayana
Translation: *Sir Richard*
ISBN: 8170262240
Price: Rs. 95.00

Northanger Abbey
Author: *Jane Austen*
ISBN: 9788170262350
Price: Rs. 75.00

Pride and Prejudice
Author: *Jane Austen*
ISBN: 9788170262459
Price: Rs. 75.00

Heart of Darkness
Author: *Joseph Conrad*
ISBN: 978170262305
Price: Rs. 50.00

Thus Spake Zarathustra
Author: *Friedrich Nietzsche*
ISBN: 8170262208
Price: Rs. 75.00

The Little Prince
Author: *Saint-Exupery*
ISBN: 8170262259
Price: Rs. 60.00

The Great Gatsby
Author: *Scott Fitzgerald*
ISBN: 9788170262336
Price: Rs. 60.00

Wuthering Heights
Author: *Emily Bronte*
ISBN: 8170262216
Price: Rs. 75.00

Homage to Catalonia
Author: *George Orwell*
ISBN: 8170262105
Price: Rs. 75.00

Nineteen Eighty Four
Author: *George Orwell*
ISBN: 817026202X
Price: Rs. 75.00

Siddhartha
Author: *Hermann Hesse*
ISBN: 9788170262428
Price: Rs. 75.00

Macbeth
Author: *Shakespeare*
ISBN: 9788170262381
Price: Rs. 50.00